P9-CEU-451

THE
EVERYTHING KIDS'®
MAGICAL
SCIENCE EXPERIMENTS BOOK

Dazzle your friends and family with dozens of science tricks!

Tom Robinson
Puzzles by Beth L. Blair

A adamsmedia
Avon, Massachusetts

DEDICATION
For Matt and Megan

EDITORIAL
Innovation Director: Paula Munier
Editorial Director: Laura M. Daly
Associate Copy Chief: Sheila Zwiebel
Acquisitions Editor: Kerry Smith
Development Editor: Brett Palana-Shanahan
Production Editor: Casey Ebert

PRODUCTION
Director of Manufacturing: Susan Beale
Production Project Manager: Michelle Roy Kelly
Prepress: Erick DaCosta, Matt LeBlanc
Interior Layout: Heather Barrett,
Brewster Brownville, Colleen Cunningham,
Jennifer Oliveira

Copyright ©2007, F+W Publications, Inc. All rights reserved. This book, or parts thereof, may not be reproduced in any form without permission from the publisher; exceptions are made for brief excerpts used in published reviews and photocopies made for classroom use.

An Everything® Series Book.
Everything® and everything.com® are registered trademarks of F+W Publications, Inc.

Published by Adams Media, an F+W Publications Company
57 Littlefield Street, Avon, MA 02322. U.S.A.
www.adamsmedia.com

ISBN 10: 1-59869-426-X
ISBN 13: 978-1-59869-426-0

Printed in the United States of America.

J I H G F E D C B A

This publication is designed to provide accurate and authoritative information with regard to the subject matter covered. It is sold with the understanding that the publisher is not engaged in rendering legal, accounting, or other professional advice. If legal advice or other expert assistance is required, the services of a competent professional person should be sought.
　　　　　　　　　—From a *Declaration of Principles* jointly adopted by a Committee of the American Bar Association and a Committee of Publishers and Associations

Many of the designations used by manufacturers and sellers to distinguish their products are claimed as trademarks. When those designations appear in this book and Adams Media was aware of a trademark claim, the designations have been printed with initial capital letters.

Note: All activities in this book should be performed with adult supervision. Likewise common sense and care are essential to the conduct of any and all activities described in this book. Parents or guardians should supervise children. Neither the author nor the publisher assumes any responsibility for any injuries or damages arising from any activities or outings.

Cover illustrations by Dana Regan. Interior illustrations by Kurt Dolber. Puzzles by Beth L. Blair.

This book is available at quantity discounts for bulk purchases. For information, please call 1-800-289-0963.

See the entire Everything® series at *www.everything.com*.

Contents

Introduction

Would you pay a lot of money to see a scientist do experiments? Probably not. Now if it were a magician, that might be a different story. Magicians awe people. They do things that seem impossible. Their tricks defy any explanation and as hard as the audience tries to figure out how they work, they often cannot. For many, science works in the same way. They see the strange and the unexpected, and when they can't explain it, they assume that science is magic. But there is one big difference between science and magic. That difference is what makes science something everyone can do, while magic is usually left to the professionals.

What is this one difference between the two disciplines? A scientist wants to know why things work the way they do. And so does a magician. The difference is that a scientist wants others to know, also. As a result, when a scientist learns an answer to a question, he often writes a report, explaining what his original question was, what he did to test the question, and what the answer was.

Magicians never reveal their secrets. That is, magicians want you to believe that what they are doing is magic, that it cannot be explained in simple terms. Scientists, on the other hand, believe that everything has an explanation, and are happy to share that explanation with anyone who will listen.

In this book, you will be exploring a number of "magical" experiments. Many produce results that are unexpected, surprising, and initially unexplainable. But this is a science book, not a magic book. You will be shown the science behind the apparent magic, so that you can pass it along to others. You will also be challenged to take your newfound knowledge to a deeper level, by asking questions that will let you explore the concepts you are learning. At the end of each chapter, you will find an idea for a science-fair project, which is really just a more complete science experiment that you could perform over the course of a few days, weeks, or months.

As you begin, think about science as the search for explanations of common and not-so-common experiences. By the time you finish this book, you should clearly see the difference between the magic of a trained professional and the science you can do in your own home.

The experiments are organized into common themes. Each experiment is preceded by a question, which then leads to a process known as the Scientific Method. This process allows questions to lead to investigations, which lead to results, conclusions, and possibly, new questions.

The Scientific Method includes five important parts:

1. Ask a question about something that happens in the world around you.
2. Make up a possible explanation for this event. This is called a *hypothesis*.
3. Design an experiment to test your hypothesis.
4. Complete the experiment and record your results.
5. Analyze your results and use them to come to a conclusion about your hypothesis.

Scientists have been using this method for centuries to explore the magical and mysterious things they see around them. Now it's your turn—let the adventure begin!

Chapter 1

Try It, You'll Like It!

Is either of your parents a good cook? Are you? For many kids, the idea of making an actual meal is a little scary. And yet, you still like to eat. So let's explore some of the magic that you can find when working with food. In this chapter you'll learn about killer straws, edible invisible ink, trained raisins, and how to make a soda fountain with a twist.

SAFETY NOTE: Make sure whenever you work with food as part of your science experiments that you do not eat the food after you are done, unless you are specifically instructed to do so. It may be interesting to work with, but it could be dangerous if you tried to eat it.

Try This: Killer Straw

No, this isn't going to involve committing a crime, nor will it require a police investigation. This experiment simply demonstrates the magic of air, and the strength it provides to otherwise flimsy materials. The next time you are asked to pierce an unsuspecting piece of fruit, you'll be glad you know this trick.

Question: Can you use a drinking straw to cut through a raw potato?

Materials
- **Several plastic drinking straws**
- **1 fresh potato**

Procedure
1. Hold the straw about halfway between the ends, between your thumb and first two fingers, as if you were holding a pencil. Try not to squeeze it shut.
2. Gently push the straw into the side of the potato. It should not get far before the straw bends.
3. Now hold the straw at one end, between your thumb and middle finger, placing your forefinger over the end of the straw.
4. Try once again to push the straw into the potato in one swift motion.

Try It, You'll Like It!

The Science Behind the Magic

This is a story about air and what it can do. The magic lies in the fact that while the first attempt to pierce the skin of the potato failed, the second time, it worked very successfully. Why is this? It has to do with the air trapped inside the straw. When you first tried this experiment, there was a place for the air to go—out the top of the straw—making the straw itself weak. But when you placed your finger over the end, the air inside the straw was trapped. And as you tried to pierce the side of the potato, all that air inside the straw made the straw rigid and very strong. It magically turned into a "killer straw."

Follow-Up

You might want to try this experiment with other fruits or vegetables. Some possible ideas include:

- **An apple**
- **An orange**
- **A pear**
- **A banana**
- **A piece of uncooked broccoli or cauliflower**
- **A tomato**

Among the fruits and vegetables for which this experiment worked, what characteristics do they have in common?

_____

_____

_____

_____

_____

_____

Science Online

Did you know that air has weight? In fact, it weighs quite a bit! Visit this NASA site to learn more about air and air pressure: *http://kids.earth.nasa.gov/archive/air_pressure/index.html*.

Science Quote

"The sun, with all those planets revolving around it and dependent on it, can still ripen a bunch of grapes as if it had nothing else in the universe to do."

—*Galileo Galilei, the "father of modern astronomy"*

Try This:
Changing Salt to Sugar

Most people can tell the difference between salty foods, like potato chips and French fries, and sweet foods, like cake and cookies. And no one would pour sugar on their French fries, or mix a large amount of salt into a batch of cookies. But what if you could change salt into sugar? Now that would be magic!

Question: Can salt be changed into sugar?

Materials
- **1 small plate**
- **1 teaspoon**
- **Salt**
- **Flour**

Science Online

Visit the Salt Institute to get answers to your burning questions about salt at *www.saltinstitute.org/4.html.*

1. Pour the salt onto the small plate.
2. Dip a wet finger into the salt and taste it to confirm its saltiness.
3. Pour the flour onto the salt and mix the two together.
4. Using the teaspoon, scoop up some of the mixture and place it on your tongue.
5. Wait a few seconds and then taste it.

The Science Behind the Magic

This is an example of a chemical reaction. When flour encounters your saliva (the wet stuff in your mouth), it gets converted into sugar, which has a sweet taste and can then be digested and used by your body. This process will happen naturally even without salt. But the presence of salt only speeds up the process so the magic happens more quickly.

Try It, You'll Like It!

Did You Know?

In the year 2000, the average American consumed 152 pounds of sugar. That equals nearly a half a pound each day!

Follow-Up

Many foods you eat already contain sugar, and that doesn't mean just cookies and candy. For example, fructose is a naturally occurring form of sugar found in fruit. Research foods that contain the most natural sugar and explore the different types of sugar they contain.

WORDS to KNOW

CHEMICAL REACTION: A reaction in which the chemical structure of molecules is changed, producing new materials.

FRUCTOSE: A form of sugar found in honey and fruits, such as apples, grapes, and oranges.

Almost Impossible

Here's some more color "magic." Color in each word as directed. Ask a friend to look at each word and say the color of the letters. What happens? EXTRA FUN: Give this quiz to three different friends. How many could do it right the first time?

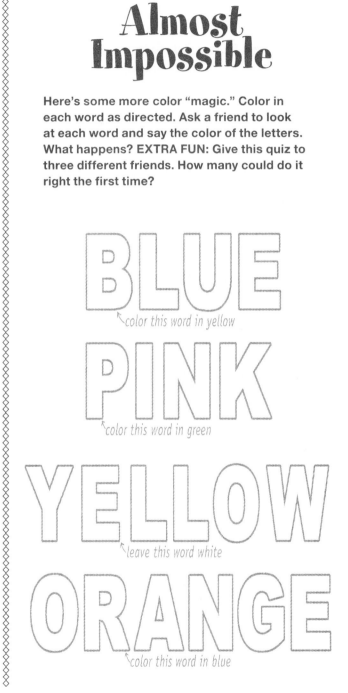

BLUE
↖ color this word in yellow

PINK
↖ color this word in green

YELLOW
↖ leave this word white

ORANGE
↖ color this word in blue

Invisible Ink

Question: How can you use food to send a hidden message?

Experiment Overview

Spy movies are famous for showing messages written in invisible ink. To the untrained eye, the message is impossible to see and read. But when the recipient exposes the message to the correct materials, it magically appears. How is this kind of thing possible?

In this experiment, you'll explore how certain types of liquids can make messages that, for a time, remain invisible. Afterward, you'll be able to test other liquids to see if they can produce the same kind of hidden message.

Science Concept

Writing a message in lemon juice, which is practically transparent, renders it invisible on the page. Only when exposed to heat, which turns the message color to brown, is the message revealed. Why does this happen? It's because of something that is found in all living objects—carbon. Molecules containing carbon atoms are nearly clear when they are dissolved in liquids. But when exposed to heat, the molecules let go of their carbon atoms, leaving them on their own. And left alone, carbon atoms are a brownish color.

KIDS' LAB LESSONS

- **Approximately ¼ cup of lemon juice (more if you want to write a long message)**

- **Cotton swab or fine-tipped paintbrush**
- **Several sheets of white paper**
- **Lamp with a light bulb that can be exposed**

Procedure

1. Dip the cotton swab in the lemon juice and begin writing your "secret" message on a white sheet of paper.
2. Allow the message to dry. While you are waiting, you might want to write some other test messages.
3. Once the message has dried, check to see that it is invisible.
4. Turn on the lamp and bring the hidden message near the bulb until the message begins to be revealed.

Questions for the Scientist

1. What sort of liquid is lemon juice? What does it taste like?

   _____

2. What did you do to cause the message to become visible?

   _____

3. If you remove the message from the heat of the bulb, do you think the message will become invisible again?

   _____

Follow-Up

Now that you have tried this experiment with lemon juice, try it with other liquids. You may already know that lemon juice is called an *acid*. This is partly what gives it its sour taste. Other common household food acids include vinegar and orange juice. Try using these liquids to see if you can create hidden messages with them. You might also try other liquids, such as milk, or other fruit juices or drinks.

No One Can See

Some parts of this riddle are invisible! Can you fill in all the vacant vowels?

The silly answer to the riddle can only be seen after you connect the dots below. When you're done, draw a small circle around the dot with no number.

WH_T   D_   P_GS   _SE
T_   WR_T_
T_P   S_CR_T   M_SS_G_S?

Try This: Swimming Raisins

You probably have friends who have trained their pets to do tricks. Some may have dogs that can roll over, catch a ball in their mouth, or play dead. Others might have cats that can meow on command, or birds that can speak several sentences. Some people even claim that they can train their fish to swim upside down, but most people don't consider that "swimming," if you know what I mean.

Yes, all of these are worthy accomplishments, but just wait until you tell your friends that you own trained raisins! They will watch in amazement as your "pets" perform feats of skill even their pets wouldn't dream of attempting.

Question: Can raisins be trained to swim and dive?

Materials
- **1 (12-ounce) can of clear soda (lemon-lime, ginger ale, club soda, or similar)**
- **Tall, clear drinking glass**
- **Several raisins**

Procedure
1. Open the can of soda and pour it all into the glass.
2. One at a time, drop the raisins into the glass and watch to see what happens.

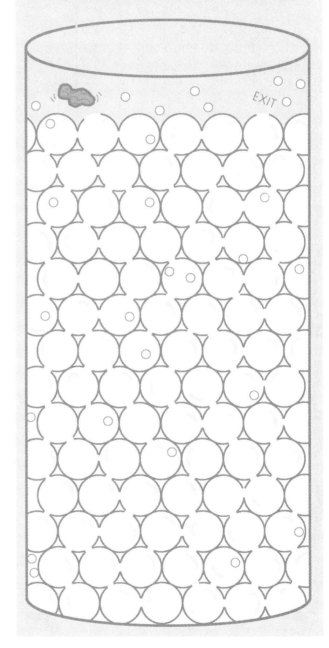

Down and Up

Get the raisin through the bubbles, from the top of the glass to the bottom, and back up again!

Try It, You'll Like It!

The Science Behind the Magic

This really isn't magic at all. Carbonated sodas contain a gas called carbon dioxide (the carbon is where the word "carbonated" comes from). When you pour the soda into the glass, the bubbles you see are bubbles of carbon dioxide being released from the soda and drifting up to the surface.

When you drop the raisins into the glass, at first they sink to the bottom because they are denser than the soda. This is the same thing that would happen if you dropped a rock into the glass. However, while the raisin rests on the bottom of the glass, the carbon dioxide bubbles gather on its skin. When enough of the bubbles (which are less dense than the soda, and therefore tend to float to the surface of the drink) gather on the skin of the raisin, it begins to float upward.

At the surface of the drink, the carbon dioxide bubbles burst, and the raisin sinks back down to the bottom of the glass. This process repeats as long as there is carbon dioxide gas remaining in the drink. You should be able to watch your "trained" raisins dive and swim in the soda for some time.

Follow-Up

This experiment should work with other objects. Can you think of some you might test out? You might try small pieces of uncooked pasta, small berries, and even very small rocks. Can you think of any others to try? Challenge yourself to find out which characteristics of the objects you test lead to the same results as that of the raisins.

What principle does this experiment demonstrate in the real world? How can people, particularly small children, take advantage of this principle when they go swimming?

_____

_____

_____

The principle in this experiment is *buoyancy.* It is what determines whether or not something floats. Small children learning to swim often wear little tubes around their arms or swim rings around their waists to stay afloat. Those air-filled rings serve the same purpose as the carbon dioxide bubbles in the Swimming Raisins experiment. The difference is that the rings don't burst at the surface of the water. As a result, the children can stay afloat.

A Milky Way to Paint

Question: Can you make colorful art in a pan of milk?

Experiment Overview

Many painters use a palette to keep their colors. A palette allows them to have all their various colors available for use, but kept separate so they don't mix. You can make a paint palette of your own by using whole milk and food coloring. But watch out—if you add liquid detergent to the mix, a mix is exactly what you get. Once you see how the mixing occurs, you can begin to experiment with different colors in different patterns to produce new "paintings."

Science Concept

Whole milk contains milk fat. This fat is usually homogenized, or spread evenly throughout the milk. When you add the drops of food coloring, which is mostly water, the colors sit in the milk in small pools. They do not mix. However, when you add liquid soap, the magic starts. As the soap spreads, its particles mix with the milk's fat particles. As this occurs, the fat begins to move around with the soap. This in turn moves the food coloring around as well. As the food coloring mixes with the white milk, your color palette will slowly turn into a painting of swirled colors.

Materials

- **1 cup homogenized whole milk**
- **Dinner or pie plate or shallow pan**
- **Food coloring of various colors**
- **Liquid dish soap**

Procedure

1. Pour the milk into the plate or pan so that it is about ½ inch deep.
2. Pour 2–3 drops of food coloring in various places around the plate.
   Be sure to use a variety of colors in order to produce a more interesting mix.
3. Add one tablespoon of dish soap to the middle of the plate.
4. Wait and watch what happens!

Questions for the Scientist

1. Why do you think the food coloring stays where it is (doesn't mix with the milk) when you first add it?

   _____

   _____

   _____

   _____

2. Why do you think the soap mixes with the milk?

   _____

   _____

   _____

   _____

3. Describe the pattern of colors that formed when you added the dish soap.

   _____

   _____

   _____

   _____

4. After a certain period of time, the colors stop swirling and mixing. What makes them stop?

   _____

   _____

   _____

   _____

Follow-Up

Try this experiment again using different combinations of colors. You can even hold a contest with your friends to see who can produce the most impressive works of art. Also try using different quantities of food coloring. Try to determine whether using more or less coloring produces a better work of art.

You might also try using different kinds of milk, including 2%, nonfat, buttermilk, chocolate or strawberry milk, and cream. Does the fat content really make a difference in the swirling effect of the colors? Are the results different if you change the color of the milk?

Science Fair: Soda Fountain

One of the more popular demonstrations to be shown in recent years involves a 2-liter bottle of soda and Mentos candies. This experiment produces an incredible display as the candies are dropped into the bottle and the soda seems to explode out of the top. Whether or not you have seen this demonstration, as a scientist you should ask yourself what could possibly cause this kind of reaction. Is it truly an explosion? Is it a release of gas somehow? Is it possible that the candies themselves act like tiny explosives, and are then expelled as a bullet would be out of a rifle?

In this project, you will explore the nature of this reaction and will determine which factors influence the outcome the most. Caution: this experiment can be very messy, and potentially dangerous if you get too close to it, so it should only be performed outdoors under adult supervision. In addition, if you use soda with sugar in it, it may make for a sticky mess to clean up. You should wear eye protection when performing this experiment.

Question: How do you make a REAL soda fountain?

Experiment Overview

The demonstration itself is fairly simple. It involves dropping a fixed number of the Mentos candies into the mouth of a 2-liter bottle of soda and watching the results. But as a scientist, you will be exploring the variables that determine the extent of the reaction, and will be testing several different combinations to find the best one. One of the key parts of any successful experiment is replication, or doing it over and over so you can be sure of your results.

Science Concept

As you saw earlier, carbonated soda contains carbon dioxide gas. When the bottle is opened, the gas is allowed to escape via the bubbles in the soda. You saw earlier how raisins can be made to "swim" by riding these bubbles to the top. But something completely different happens when the candies are dropped into the bottle. The candies are made with a very special outer coating. This outer coating has a large number of tiny pits in it, which allow the carbon dioxide gas bubbles to collect. But that's not all. The ingredients that go into the candy shell react with the sugar in the soda to produce a dramatic reaction that results in the explosive fountain of soda that comes out of the top of the bottle.

Just what is this reaction? It has to do with the ingredients in the candy. As the candy dissolves in the soda, the gelatin and gum arabic in it break the tension in the soda molecules. This allows the carbon dioxide bubbles to be released more quickly than usual. In addition, the surface of the candies contains tiny pits where carbon dioxide gas bubbles can collect. The candies are heavier than the soda, and tend to sink to the bottom of the bottle. Very quickly, this combination of gas buildup and release of surface tension

Try It, You'll Like It!

in the molecules produces the incredible fountain of soda.

In this science fair experiment, your task is to find a way to measure the effect of the fountain. You might decide to measure the height of the fountain, or you might measure the amount of soda remaining in the bottle after the eruption. Just go beyond simply measuring the effect of one reaction. You should try different forms of the same soda. For example, try a sugar-free version of the same flavor. If a caffeine-free version is available, try that. You can also try different brands of the same flavor.

Additionally, you can try changing candies while you keep the brand of soda the same. You might try different flavors of Mentos candies, or you might even try different brands of candies. What's most important is that whenever you change a variable, you change only one at a time. Either the brand of soda should change, or the amount of sugar in the soda should change, or the type of candy you test should change. Be careful in your measurements and you will have an explosive science-fair experiment. You may wish to videotape the results as a way to document your observations.

Materials

- **Several 2-liter bottles of soda. They may include soda with sugar, sugar-free, caffeine-free, or other combinations you would like to test.**
- **Packages of Mentos mint candies**
- **Other types of round candies for comparison if you wish**
- **Test tube or other similar device for holding a package of Mentos candies**
- **One 3" x 5" note card**
- **Meter stick**
- **Measuring cup**
- **Protective eye goggles**

Procedure

The following procedures are appropriate for any trial of this experiment. Substitute the specific soda type and candy type you have chosen:

1. Open a package of the candies and fill the test tube with the whole package.
2. Open the 2-liter bottle of soda and place on a flat surface out in the open. This experiment MUST be completed outdoors.
3. Put on your goggles for protection.
4. Place the note card over the open end of the test tube. Hold the card firmly in place as you carefully turn the test tube over so that its opening faces down.
5. Now, you need to decide how to measure the results of your experiment. If you are going to measure the height of the fountain, be sure to have a way to measure that height already

in place. This might mean you perform the experiment near a wall so you can mark the maximum height on the wall. Enlist the help of a spotter to note the height of the fountain. If you are going to measure the amount of soda remaining in the bottle after the experiment, do that after the test is complete.

6. Place the test tube, open end down, over the top of the bottle. In one motion, remove the card and allow the candies to fall into the bottle.

7. Quickly back out of the way and observe your own personal soda fountain.

Questions for the Scientist

1. What combination of candy and soda produced the tallest fountain?

   _____
   _____
   _____

2. What combination of candy and soda left the least soda behind in the bottle?

   _____
   _____
   _____

3. What was the range of heights produced by your various soda fountains?

   _____
   _____
   _____

4. What was the range in amounts of soda left behind in the bottle?

   _____
   _____
   _____

5. What sort of difference did you notice in the reactions produced by sodas with sugar and without sugar?

   _____
   _____
   _____

6. How else could you possibly have measured the reaction you produced?

   _____
   _____
   _____

7. Can you think of any implication for the results of this experiment in your everyday life? That is, are there certain types of foods that you would be less inclined to mix as a result of this experiment?

   _____
   _____
   _____

Conclusion

In some situations, the ingredients in one type of food item react in a special way with the ingredients in another food item. This is one of those situations. The reaction you produced demonstrates that mixing this particular kind of candy with soda that contains sugar could be dangerous. Learning this lesson in a controlled, scientific setting is probably better, and safer, than learning it by eating these food together. Keep your eyes open for other foods that might react in a dangerous way.

Chapter 2

Running Hot and Cold

What is summer like where you live? Is it hot and humid? Do you wish you had a personal air conditioner you could carry with you wherever you go? What about winter? Are the streets continually covered with snow and ice, and do the cloudy, cold days seem to last forever?

One of the most remarkable changes that takes place over the course of a year, no matter where you live, is the change in seasons. From the hot, summer days, to the cold, wintry nights, the changes in hot and cold weather always make us take note of the changing seasons.

The act of heating something up or cooling it down often produces surprising results.

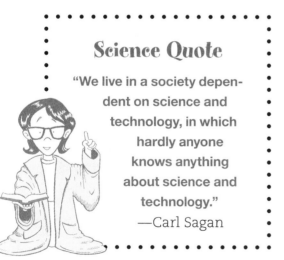

Science Quote

"We live in a society dependent on science and technology, in which hardly anyone knows anything about science and technology."
—Carl Sagan

In this chapter, you will explore the effects of heating and cooling different materials and the magic that happens when you do. In this chapter, you'll explore the magic of exploding ice, floating water, sharp string, and rising dough.

Try This: Exploding Water

One of the well-known "facts" about heating and cooling materials is that when things heat up, they expand, and when they cool down, they shrink. As an example, if you were to try to open a jar of spaghetti sauce whose lid was tightly sealed, you might run the lid under hot water. The heat of the water causes the lid to expand just enough to make it easier to open the lid.

Cold to Hot???

Add enough heat to cold water and it turns into something completely different — it seems like magic! Follow the directions below to see what you end up with. On the lines provided, write the letters you get after completing each step.

WATER

turn W upside-down _____

move M to the end _____

move T to the start _____

switch A and E _____

change R to S _____

move S to the start _____

That's cool! Oops, I mean hot!

Similarly, you might notice little cracks in the sidewalks near your house. These are put there on purpose, and they are called expansion joints. In the summer, the concrete usually expands and the cracks are thin. But in the winter, the cracks tend to open wider as the concrete shrinks. But does cooling things always make them shrink?

WORDS to KNOW

EXPANSION JOINT: A crack or gap intentionally placed in objects like sidewalks and roads that allow the material to expand and shrink in different temperatures without causing the road or sidewalk to buckle.

Question: Can you "explode" a bottle of water by freezing it?

Materials
- **A 500-mL bottle of drinking water**
- **Freezer**
- **Marking pen**

Procedure
1. Stand the bottle on a counter and mark the height of the water. There should be a small amount of air between the surface of the water and the cap.
2. Place the bottle upright in the freezer and let it sit for at least three hours.
3. Take the bottle out of the freezer and notice how the water height has changed.

The Science Behind the Magic
This seems to be a magical result, but it's not. Water is an unusual substance in that as it freezes, instead of shrinking, as you might expect it to do, it actually expands. This is because of the air that is stored in the water as a liquid. That air expands as the water freezes into ice, and that makes the ice take up more room than the water did. Your bottle may have been distorted slightly, as the ice caused the bottle to expand.

One consequence of this process is that the same amount of water (H_2O) takes up more space. The term that describes this relationship between amount of material and amount of space it takes up is *density*. The more material there is in the same space, the more dense the material is. On the other hand, if you have the same amount of something, but it takes up more space, it is less dense. When the water freezes and expands to form ice, the same amount of material takes up more space and therefore, it is less dense.

This change explains how ice cubes can float in a glass of water. Since ice is less dense than water, it floats. This is similar to how icebergs, which are really just huge, floating chunks of ice, can float in the ocean.

Follow-Up

What do you think would happen if you heated up that bottle of water? You have to be careful, because if you heat it too much, the plastic bottle might melt. But here is another place you can see this result. If you have a thermometer at home, the kind you take your temperature with when you are not feeling well, you may be able to explore this. It needs to be the kind that is made of glass, with a thin line of red liquid showing the temperature. When you stick the thermometer in your mouth, the red liquid in the base of the thermometer expands and climbs up the tube until it stops at the temperature of your mouth.

Can you think of any other examples of liquids expanding or shrinking when you heat or cool them? What about objects that are solid? See if you can find five examples of objects that shrink or expand when heated or cooled.

Did You Know?

Salt is often used on roads and sidewalks as a de-icer. What it does is lower the freezing temperature of the ice. This means that ice made from pure water that has frozen at 32° Fahrenheit may turn to water at that same temperature when mixed with salt.

Science Online

This site explores the world of icebergs, and takes a look at the collision that caused the *Titanic* to sink in 1912: *http://oceanworld.tamu.edu/students/iceberg*.

Try This:
Hanging by a Thread

Ice can be slippery. In the winter, when it snows, the roads often turn icy and people have a hard time driving on it. If you have ever tried to ice skate, chances are, the first time you tried it you found out just how slick ice can be. Even picking up ice cubes can be difficult, as they tend to slip right out of your hands. So perhaps there is a better way—don't use your hands!

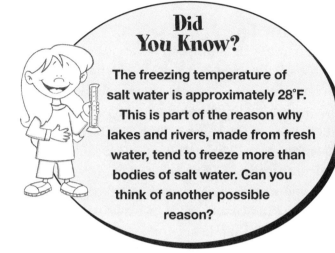

Did You Know?

The freezing temperature of salt water is approximately 28°F. This is part of the reason why lakes and rivers, made from fresh water, tend to freeze more than bodies of salt water. Can you think of another possible reason?

Question: Can you lift an ice cube without touching it?

Materials
- **Several large ice cubes, taken directly from the freezer**
- **Salt**
- **String that can be cut into pieces**
- **Scissors**
- **Paper towel**

WORDS to KNOW

MELTING POINT: The temperature at which a solid melts to form a liquid. This is also commonly called the freezing point, as it is also the temperature of the reverse change at which a liquid freezes to form a solid.

Procedure
1. Place one ice cube on the paper towel.
2. Cut a piece of string at least 12 inches long.
3. Without touching the ice cube with your hands, try to lift the ice cube using only the string.
4. Lay the string across the top of the ice cube, leaving several inches free on either side.
5. Pour salt on the ice cube, covering the top of the ice and the string.
6. Wait 3–5 minutes.
7. Lift the string from both ends and watch the magic happen.

The Science Behind the Magic

By itself, the string cannot lift the ice cube. However, salt has a special relationship with ice. When you pour salt on the ice, the ice melts slightly, and then refreezes at a slightly lower temperature. Salt water has a lower melting point than pure water. When the ice refreezes, it "captures" the string under the surface of the ice. When you lift up on the string, the ice comes with it.

Follow-Up

How much salt does it take to produce this effect? See if you can devise an experiment that will test to see how little salt you can use to still lift the ice cube. Alternately, you may want to try this experiment with ice at different temperatures. Try using ice taken straight from the freezer and compare the results to ice that has been sitting out on the counter for 5 minutes, 10 minutes, or more.

Also, if it snows where you live, the next time it happens, try pouring some salt on a small area of snow or ice and see whether or not the salt helps melt the ice.

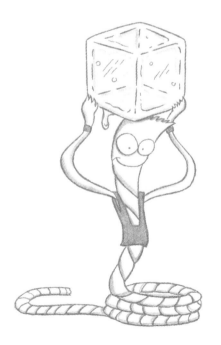

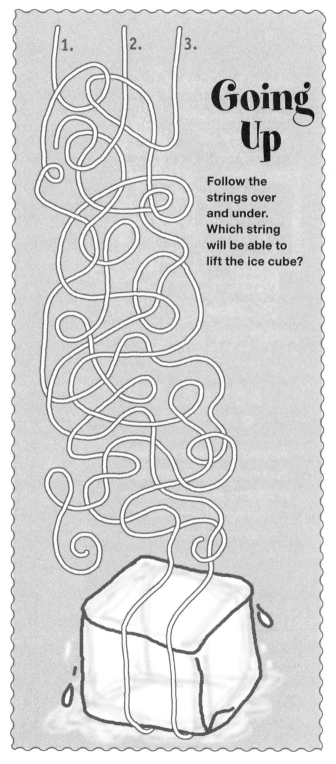

Going Up

Follow the strings over and under. Which string will be able to lift the ice cube?

Floating Water

Question: Can you make water float on oil?

Experiment Overview

In this experiment, you will first demonstrate how it is possible to make water "float" on oil by cooling it to the point that it freezes. You see, when water freezes, it expands and becomes less dense. This change is usually enough to make the density of ice less than that of the cooking oil. You will pour cooking oil and colored water into a jar and allow them to settle until one floats on top of the other. Then you will place the jar in the freezer for several hours. What you see when you remove the jar from the freezer may surprise you.

Your next task will be to test other liquid combinations to see if freezing them changes their density enough to make "heavy" liquids float.

Science Concept

The factor that determines whether or not something will float is its density. For example, a piece of wood floats in a lake because the wood's density is less than that of water. However, if you were to drop a large boulder into the lake, it sinks quickly to the bottom. The boulder's density is greater than that of water.

If you were to pour some cooking oil into a jar containing water, the oil wouldn't mix with the water. It would appear to "float" or sit on top of the water. This is because the density of cooking oil is less than that of water. This is also why you tend to see rainbows of colors where oil or gasoline has spilled on wet pavement. The oil stays on top of the water because of its lower density.

When you freeze the water, however, its density decreases to the point that the ice will actually float on top of the oil, as if it were an ice cube in a very large drink.

Materials

- Large, clear, canning jar without a lid
- Measuring cups
- Food coloring
- 1 cup of tap water
- 1 cup of cooking oil
- Other liquids for testing, such as:
    - Corn syrup
    - Pancake syrup
    - Soda
    - Molasses
    - Milk
    - Coffee

Procedure

1. Pour one cup of cooking oil into the canning jar.
2. Mix a few drops of food coloring into one cup of water until the color is easy to observe.
3. Slowly pour the colored water into the jar containing oil. Watch carefully to see how the water and oil interact. Do they mix, or do they stay separate?
4. Take note of which liquid "floats" on top of the other.
5. After clearing a spot in the freezer, place the jar in the freezer for several hours. Resist the temptation to sneak a peek while you wait.
6. When sufficient time has passed, remove the jar from the freezer and observe any changes you see.

Questions for the Scientist

1. Why don't you think the oil and water mixed when you placed them in the jar?

   _____

2. Which liquid appeared to have the lowest density? How could you tell?

   _____

3. What did you observe about your liquids when you removed the jar from the freezer? Did they look the same as when you placed them in the freezer?

   _____

   _____

4. What do you predict will happen as the ice begins to melt? Let the jar sit in the room for a period of time and observe the changes in the two liquids as the ice melts. Describe what you observe.

   _____

   _____

5. Repeat this experiment with other pairs of liquids. Think about some of these questions as you perform your experiment:
   a. Which pairs of liquids mixed together and which ones did not?
   b. What does this tell you about the densities of these pairs of liquids?
   c. Did you find any other liquids that changed positions like the water did?
   d. What characteristics do those liquids share that makes them do this?

Try This:
Collapsing Bottles

Heating and cooling air can produce results that look like magic. But you don't have to be a magician to perform this experiment. You just need to heat and cool a container of air.

Question: How do you make a bottle collapse?

Materials
- **Empty 500-mL plastic bottle**
- **Tap water**
- **Frying pan**
- **Stove**
- **Adult to assist**

Procedure
1. Fill the plastic bottle about ¼ full with tap water.
2. Fill the frying pan with about a half inch of water and turn on the burner.
3. Place the plastic bottle in the frying pan to heat up the water inside. Have your adult helper watch to make sure the plastic bottle does not begin to melt.
4. When you see steam escaping from the top of your bottle, have your adult helper place the lid tightly on the top of the bottle and remove it from the pan.
5. Place the sealed bottle on the counter and turn off the stove.
6. As the bottle cools, watch to see it collapse on itself.

The Science Behind the Magic

As you may have learned in the previous experiment, air expands when it is heated. The air in the plastic bottle was heated up on the stove. When you capped it, you prevented any air from entering or escaping the bottle. As it cooled, the air inside the bottle contracted, or took up less space. Plastic is soft enough that the bottle had to collapse to account for the reduced space taken up by the air.

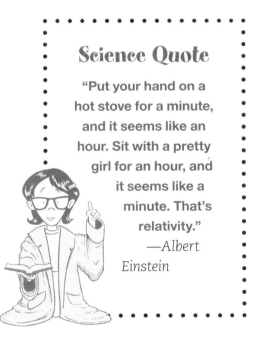

Science Quote
"Put your hand on a hot stove for a minute, and it seems like an hour. Sit with a pretty girl for an hour, and it seems like a minute. That's relativity."
—Albert Einstein

Follow-Up

You can try this experiment with metal cans, also, but only certain kinds. What must you be able to do to the cans in order for this experiment to work?

_____

_____

_____

_____

You must be able to seal the top of the can in order for this to work. For example, an empty soda can probably won't work well, as it is very difficult to seal it once it has been opened. Any can or bottle with a screw-top lid should work.

Science Quote

"True science teaches us to doubt."
—Claude Bernard, French physiologist

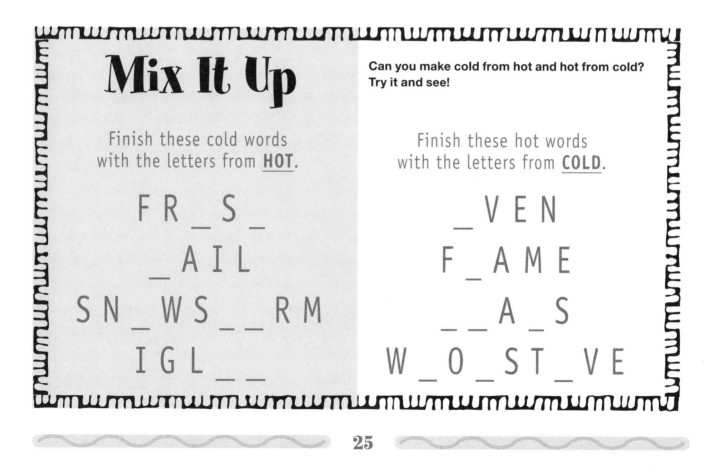

Mix It Up

Finish these cold words with the letters from **HOT**.

FR _ S _

_ AIL

SN _ WS _ _ RM

IGL _ _

Can you make cold from hot and hot from cold? Try it and see!

Finish these hot words with the letters from **COLD**.

_ VEN

F _ AME

_ _ A _ S

W _ O _ ST _ VE

String Knife

Question: Can a string cut ice?

Experiment Overview

You've already seen how a string can be used to lift a piece of ice, through the use of salt. Now you will get to "cut" through a piece of ice using only a piece of wire or string. This experiment uses gravity and time to produce the desired effects, and may take both practice and patience. But when you pull off this feat of skill, and can explain it to those around you, all your hard work will have been worth it.

Science Concept

Ice is frozen water. By itself, it tends to stay frozen, unless, of course, it is subjected to heat. But other things can cause ice to melt—pressure, for example. One theory is that ice skates operate on this principle. This theory claims that the pressure of the thin blades of the skates on the surface of the ice cause a tiny layer of the ice to melt, and the skates actually move on that thin layer of water. After the skate passes, the ice refreezes. This experiment uses pressure of a string to melt a piece of ice, move through that melted portion, and allow the ice to refreeze behind it. In so doing, the string can move its way through the ice, as if it were cutting it.

Materials

- **Several ice cubes from the freezer, the larger, the better**
- **1 empty glass bottle with a cork in its mouth**
- **1 piece of copper wire, approximately 10"–12" in length**
- **1 piece of string, approximately 10"–12" in length**
- **2 hammers or other similar weights**

Procedure

1. Remove an ice cube from the freezer and balance it on top of the cork.
2. Tie one hammer to each end of the copper wire and carefully hang the wire across the top of the ice cube.
3. Over time, the wire should begin to pass through the ice until it finally passes through completely.

Questions for the Scientist

1. What do you think caused the wire to pass through the ice?

    _____

    _____

2. Why did the ice melt above the wire as it passed through?

    _____

    _____

3. What role did the hammers play in this experiment?

    _____

    _____

4. What might have happened if you had used a different material than the copper wire? Try this experiment again using the string.

    _____

    _____

5. What might have changed in this experiment had you used a plastic bottle instead of one made from another material? Try this experiment again using a plastic bottle or an aluminum can.

    _____

    _____

Follow-Up

There is another theory about ice melting under pressure that claims it's not pressure that causes the ice to melt. Instead, this theory claims that certain materials conduct heat better than others. These materials include copper wire. As a result, it is the heat passing through the wire that causes the ice to melt, not the pressure. What does this experiment indicate to you about the truth of this theory?

To extend this experiment, try varying the weights that hang from the ice and measuring the time necessary for the wire to pass completely through the ice. Is there a weight that will not cause the wire to pass through the ice?

Science Fair: Now You're Cooking!

For centuries, bakers have sought that perfect recipe, the perfect combination of ingredients, cooking time, and chemistry to produce mouth-watering delights for all to enjoy. Sometimes, simply walking into a bakery is enough to make your stomach growl with anticipation, as the smells overwhelm you: cookies, cakes, pies, and perhaps the most comforting smell of all, the smell of freshly baked bread.

What bakers know that many of us who aren't as talented in the kitchen do not is that a perfect loaf of bread doesn't happen by accident. It often requires planning, careful measuring, patience, and one special ingredient: yeast.

Question: Do yeast cells like it hot or cold?

Experiment Overview

In this experiment, you will get to act like a real baker and make a small amount of bread dough. However, in order to test the effect of temperature on the growth rate of the yeast, you will be using water of varying temperatures and measuring the growth for each temperature. You should not attempt to eat any of the dough balls you produce—they are merely for experimentation. At the end of this experiment, you will get a recipe for making a real loaf of bread. With an adult's help, you can bring your project to a tasty conclusion!

Science Concept

Yeast typically is found in its dry form, often in a jar that can be purchased at the grocery store. This prepared form of yeast needs to be mixed with water in order to "come to life." The water allows the yeast cells to begin growing, and you usually will see this happen as the water appears to foam when yeast is mixed in. Next, the foaming water is usually mixed with a small amount of flour and then the rest of the bread dough is mixed together.

Did You Know?

You can actually use yeast to blow up a balloon without touching it. Simply pour warm water into an empty 20-ounce soda bottle and mix in an envelope of yeast. Immediately cover the mouth of the bottle with a balloon and watch it inflate as the yeast reacts with the water to form carbon dioxide gas.

Good Catch

Which is faster, hot or cold?

You don't need to use magic to learn the answer to this silly science question — all you have to do is think of the number suggested by each clue. Then, circle the word in the column with that number. For example, you have one nose. So, for the first clue, "nose," circle the word in column 1 (for 1 nose). When you are done, read the circled words from bottom to top.

	column 1	column 2	column 3
nose	COLD	COLD	HOT
arms	COLD	CATCH	MUCH
head	TO	SLOWER	ARE
twins	THAN	EASY	ALWAYS
triplets	THE	HOT	IS
thirds	IS	EXACT	IT
sun	BECAUSE	AT	SAME
double	SPEED	HOT	NIGHT

Remember to read the circled words from bottom to top!

Yeast, like most living creatures, grows best under the right combination of water and warmth. When the yeast starts to mix with the flour, the starch in the flour becomes the diet for the hungry yeast cells. As they feed, they give off carbon dioxide (similar to the bubbles you would find in a can of soda) and alcohol. The flour then captures this gas, and forms tiny pockets of air. As these air pockets increase and grow, the dough rises and fills out into its final shape for baking.

You might be wondering whether anything can speed up or slow down the process by which yeast reacts to make bread rise. The answer is yes. Salt actually slows down the reaction, while sugar speeds it up. Often, bakers will use combinations of salt and sugar to regulate the rate of rising of their breads or rolls. But even more than the ingredients used, temperature probably has the largest effect on the rate at which bread dough rises. Using water that is too hot or too cold can significantly reduce the effect of the yeast. In addition, the outside temperature during the rising can also greatly affect your results. This experiment will give you several different ways to measure the effects of these factors on the rising of bread dough that has been leavened by yeast.

Materials

NOTE: This set of ingredients will produce a single ball of bread dough. As you create different test doughs, you will simply modify one or more of these quantities.

- **100 grams (3.5 ounces) white flour**
- **Dash of salt**
- **1 teaspoon white sugar**
- **¼ envelope dry yeast (about ½ teaspoon)**
- **50 mL (1.69 ounces) water**
- **Measuring spoons**
- **Glass measuring cup (one that measures up to 2 cups)**
- **Mixing bowl**
- **Bowl for holding the completed dough**
- **Kitchen or paper towel**
- **Ruler or other measuring device**
- **Teaspoon (for stirring)**
- **Candy/Deep frying thermometer**
- **Notebook for recording data**

Procedure

1. Select at least four temperatures for the water you will use in this experiment. Some options are:

- **Water that has been sitting at room temperature for at least 30 minutes**
- **Water taken directly from the refrigerator**
- **Water that has been placed in the freezer, but has not yet frozen**
- **Water that has been heated in the microwave for one minute**
- **Water from an "Instant Hot" faucet**
- **Water that has been left outside on a warm day**

2. Measure the temperature of your water and record it in your notebook.
3. Pour 50 mL of your chosen water into the measuring cup and slowly mix in the dry yeast until it dissolves or begins to foam.
4. In the mixing bowl, pour half of the flour and mix in the yeast mixture until a wet dough forms.
5. Add the salt, sugar, and the remaining flour and mix thoroughly until a smooth dough forms.
6. Remove the dough from the mixing bowl and form into a ball with your hands. Carefully measure the diameter of your dough ball and record it in your data notebook.
7. Place the dough ball in bowl, cover with a towel and set on the counter.
8. Repeat steps 2–7 with each of the differ-

Science Online

You can read about 150 years of yeast history, courtesy of Fleischmann's: *www .breadworld.com/science history/science.asp.*

ent temperatures of water you have chosen to test in this experiment. When you have completed this stage, you should have several bowls of rising dough.

9. Let the dough balls sit out for at least four hours (overnight works best) and then carefully measure the diameter of each dough ball to see which one grew the largest.

Questions for the Scientist

1. What temperature was the most effective for causing your bread to rise? Why do you think this temperature worked best?

_____

2. Could you detect any smells coming from your bread? What did it smell like? What do you suppose caused those smells?

_____

3. What might have happened if you had let the dough sit for a longer period of time, several days for example?

_____

4. Research ideal water temperature for rising bread dough to see how closely your results agreed with that recommended temperature.

_____

Did You Know?

During the Passover feast, Jewish believers eat only unleavened bread. That means it was not made with any leavening (rising) ingredients, such as yeast. The result is typically a flat, crisp bread.

Follow-Up

There are several variations to this experiment that you could also perform. For example, you could use water that is always the same temperature and you could vary the temperature at the place you left the dough to rise. You could place one dough ball on the counter, one in the refrigerator, one in the freezer; one could go outside, and one could go in the oven with the door open and light on (but no heat). In this form of experiment, instead of testing the effects of water temperature on the rising of bread dough, you would be testing the effects of the air temperature.

Another possibility would be to keep both water and air temperatures the same, but vary the amount of salt or the amount of sugar you add to the dough. Since salt and sugar are known to either speed up or slow down the yeast's ability to grow, changing the amount of salt or sugar (but never both in the same experiment) would give you another possible question to explore.

It's always important, however, when doing these types of experiments that you only change one variable at a time. To summarize the possibilities discussed here, you should choose one of the following variables to change, and therefore study:

- **Temperature of the water**
- **Air temperature**
- **Amount of salt added**
- **Amount of sugar added**

Can you think of any others?

Conclusion

Yeast is a remarkable ingredient. Many of the baked goods you eat use some form of leavening, whether it is yeast, baking powder, or something else. You might even want to try baking cookies, or a cake, without adding baking powder, to see what happens. Many prepackaged mixes already include these ingredients, so you don't have to worry about it. But if you bake from scratch, be sure to include them if having your work rise is important to you.

Simple Bread Recipe
(courtesy of Lisa Robinson)

Ingredients
- 1½ cups warm water (110°F)
- 1 tablespoon active dry yeast
- 2 tablespoons white sugar
- 2 tablespoons vegetable oil
- 1 teaspoon salt
- 4 cups bread flour

Instructions
1. In a bowl, mix together water, yeast, and sugar. Let stand until it becomes creamy. It should take about 10 minutes.
2. Add the oil, salt, and 2 cups flour. Mix in the remaining flour ½ cup at a time.
3. Dump the dough onto a lightly floured flat surface and knead it until it is smooth and slightly springy. Do this for 5–10 minutes.
4. Dump dough into a greased bowl and cover the bowl with a damp cloth. Place the bowl in a warm location and let it sit for one hour. The dough should approximately double in size.
5. Remove dough from the bowl and knead it again for two minutes before splitting the dough and placing the halves in two loaf pans that have been coated with oil or butter. Cover the pans with a damp cloth and let the dough rise for one more hour.
6. Preheat the oven to 400°F and bake your bread for 18–20 minutes, or until the edges turn golden brown.
7. Remove from oven, slice, and serve.

Chapter 3
Life in a Fun House

Who hasn't been forced to do chores by their parents? Some days it seems like all parents care about is doing chores. Why can't they just relax and enjoy themselves for an evening, and let you do the same? Then again, it is nice to eat dinner on clean plates, and have clean clothes, and not to have to step over garbage to get to the front door, so maybe chores aren't the worst way to spend your time. But what if you could make your chores into interesting, even magical, science experiments?

There's no guarantee that doing chores will ever be a task you would consider "fun," but there are probably items lying around your house that, in your capable hands, could produce some interesting activities. See what you can find in your "fun" house. In this chapter, you'll explore racing toothpicks, balancing candles, magic bouncing balls, and metal in cereal.

Try This: Racing Toothpicks

See if you can find a hiding place where your family keeps toothpicks. If so, then you are ready for a racing game to see just how fast you can make them go in water. But be careful—you don't want to make a big mess that you'll have to clean up afterward.

Did You Know?

The Basilisk lizard is a creature that can literally walk on water. It uses the water's surface tension to support itself as it runs on two legs across the surface of water. For this talent, it has been nicknamed "The Jesus Lizard."

Question: Can you make toothpicks race through water?

Materials
- Several toothpicks
- Aluminum pie pan or similar
- Water
- Liquid detergent

Procedure
1. Fill the pan with enough water to float the toothpicks.
2. Arrange toothpicks on the surface of the water in the shape of your choice. You

WORDS to KNOW

SURFACE TENSION: A force that keeps water molecules stuck together near the water's surface.

might want to try a triangle, a square, or a pentagon. Be sure to lay the ends of each toothpick across the ends of another, so they don't float away.

3. Take one additional toothpick and dip one end in the liquid detergent.

4. Carefully place the soapy end of the extra toothpick as close as possible to the center of the arranged toothpicks in the pan.

5. The toothpicks should shoot out of formation.

The Science Behind the Magic

This experiment demonstrates the surface tension of water. At the surface of the water, the molecules are held together and this tension is what helps the toothpicks stay close together. Liquid detergent breaks that surface tension, and causes the toothpicks to move away suddenly. It doesn't take much

detergent to cause this effect, so it's possible that if you were to try this again using the same water, nothing would happen. You may have to dump the first batch of water and start again.

Follow-Up

Would you like to see your toothpicks in a race? Set up the experiment again with a fresh batch of water in the pan. Carefully place a set of "racers" in the pan all pointing toward the far end of the pan. Dip an entire toothpick in liquid detergent and drop it behind the lined-up toothpicks. Be sure to place it perpendicular to the toothpicks that will be racing. Which one moves the farthest? The fastest?

This experiment can also be done using pepper sprinkled across the surface of the water in the pan. Try it and watch the pepper scurry away!

Try This:
Personal Water Fountain

Most schools provide drinking fountains for their students. These machines pump water from the school's water supply up through a series of pipes and out a faucet. To bring the water from under the ground up to where you can drink it takes a lot of effort. But to make water flow the other direction, downward, doesn't take any effort at all, thanks to gravity. In this experiment, you will see how gravity affects water pressure and how you can produce different streams of water from the same container just by adjusting the height of the water.

Question: How does gravity affect water streaming out of a container?

Materials
- Empty 2-liter plastic soda bottle
- Scissors
- Adult helper
- Plenty of water
- Large cake pan or cookie sheet with sides

Procedure
1. Ask your adult helper to use the scissors to cut three small holes in the plastic bottle. One hole should be above the middle of the bottle, one should be near the middle, and one should be about four inches from the bottom. The holes should be about the size of a nail hole.
2. While placing your fingers over the holes, fill the bottle with tap water.
3. Place the bottle inside the cake pan so that water can stream out without spilling on the counter.
4. At the same time, remove all three fingers covering the holes and watch how the water streams out.

The Science Behind the Magic
At first it seems that the water should be streaming out the same no matter where the holes are. However, water has weight. The more water there is pressing down at the spot where the holes are, the more water pressure there is, and the faster it comes out. This is why the water coming out of the top hole doesn't flow out very fast or far. The middle hole produces a stream that moves faster than the top one, and the bottom hole has water squirting out of it very quickly.

Follow-Up
You may have read in other science experiment books about an activity where you produced layers of liquids, such as oil, water, and corn syrup. You can try that here with the added twist of watching the liquids pour out of the holes. To do this, you will

need to keep the holes covered with pieces of tape until you are ready to release the liquids. Pour enough corn syrup or pancake syrup to fill the bottle to a point above the first hole. Then pour in enough water to fill the bottle to a point above the second hole. Finally, pour in enough cooking oil to fill the bottle to a point above the third hole. Now return the bottle to the cake pan. Quickly and carefully remove the three hole covers and watch to see how these three liquids pour out. What happened?

The density of the liquids also plays a role in determining how they come out of the bottle. The cooking oil did not experience a lot of pressure, but since it is less dense than water, it came out a little faster than the water did in the first experiment. The water pouring out of the middle hole probably did about what it did before, although the cooking oil on top of it doesn't produce the same amount of pressure that water did the first time. Finally, the syrup on the bottom, despite the pressure from the water and cooking oil above it, is thicker and doesn't flow as easily as water does. As a result, it just dribbles out of the bottle.

The Amazing Race

This toothpick can race across the surface of the water to find three answers to the riddle! Read the letters along each path from START to END. Magic!

What happened when an egg, some lettuce, and a faucet ran a race?

Ironing Out Your Cereal

Question: Is There Really Metal in Cereal?

Experiment Overview

Many dry breakfast cereals claim that they are "fortified" with vitamins and minerals. But what are these important additions to your breakfast, and are they all good for you? In this experiment, you will be examining various iron-enriched cereals. Iron is a metal that is commonly found in buildings, railroads, and tools. But it is also found in your blood. You will use a magnet to dig for this metal in a bowl of cereal and will do some comparisons between different brands to identify which brand contains the largest amount of iron.

Science Concept

It may seem a little strange to think about there being pieces of metal in your cereal, no matter how small they are, but it's true. Tiny pieces of iron are added to some cereals as a way to improve blood flow. You see, iron in your blood helps your body make hemoglobin. Hemoglobin is a protein that helps your blood carry oxygen to the rest of your body. People who have low iron levels in their blood are said to be anemic, and if their iron level drops too low, their bodies begin to show signs of tiredness and lethargy.

KIDS' LAB LESSONS

Some cereal manufacturers add tiny pieces of iron, called iron filings, to their cereal. If you were to ingest large pieces of iron, it would be dangerous for you. But these tiny pieces, almost invisible, and in small amounts, actually help your blood do its job of carrying oxygen throughout your body.

Materials

- **3 cups of Total brand iron-fortified cereal**
  (**NOTE:** Total makes a number of different kinds of cereal, but all claim to be iron-fortified, so choose one you are likely to want to eat after the experiment is complete.)
- **Water**
- **Blender or large spoon**
- **Non-metallic bowl**
- **Strong bar magnet**
- **Sheet of white computer printer paper (optional)**

EXPERIMENT NOTE: A regular refrigerator magnet is not strong enough to attract the iron filings. You need to use a strong magnet, and one shaped like a bar will tend to be the most successful.

Find the Iron

It might take a bit of magic to find the one time that the word IRON is spelled correctly in this bowl of cereal! Look up and down, and side-to-side.

```
I R N O I O R N I R N O I R O I R N I R
I I R O I O N I R I R R R O R I R N
R R O I N N O O I O N I O N O O R O
O N N R N I I N R N R O R O O I O N
I O O O R I R O I R R N O R O N I R
I R R I O N N N O I R O N O O N
R O N O R O N O N R I R I N O O
  I I R O O R I O N R O R R
    O R I R R R N O O N O I
    I R R O I O N R O I
      O N R R O R
      N I R I O N
```

Procedure

1. Pour the cereal into the blender or your bowl.
2. Add enough water to cover the cereal.
3. Either blend the mixture until the cereal is completely ground up, or mash the cereal for several minutes with the spoon.
4. If you are using a blender, pour the contents of the pitcher into the non-metallic bowl. Rinse the bottom of the pitcher with water in order to capture all of the iron particles.
5. Stir your magnet through the cereal mixture. Iron is heavier than water, so the filings will tend to sink to the bottom. Be patient and thorough with your stirring.
6. Remove the magnet from the cereal and look for tiny black iron filings stuck to the magnet. They will look like pieces of stubble that you might find on a man's face if he hasn't shaved.
7. To see the iron pieces more clearly, rub the magnet against a sheet of white paper, such as what you might find in a computer printer.

Questions for the Scientist

1. Why should you use iron-fortified cereal to perform this experiment?

   _____

   _____

2. What purpose do you think the water served in this experiment?

   _____

   _____

3. Do you think your results would have been different had you used milk instead of water?

   _____

   _____

4. How do you feel about eating cereal with pieces of iron in it? Are you more likely to eat cereal like this, less likely, or just as likely?

   _____

Follow-Up

The brand of cereal you chose to test is not the only brand that has iron in it. Visit a grocery store and find other cereals that contain iron. Look to see if any of them provide "100% of the Recommended Daily Allowance" of iron. You can buy these cereals and do a comparison at home by repeating the experiment with different brands to see which have more iron than others.

You may also wish to compare the cereals that have iron in them with those that do not to see if there is anything these cereals have in common. For example, would you consider these iron-fortified cereals to be "healthy" cereals? Would you like to eat them yourself? Do you think they appeal more to adults or to kids? Part of the fun of doing science experiments is making up new questions and then finding ways to answer them.

Try This:
Blowing Out Candles

Nearly everyone has had the chance to blow out a candle before. Whether it was on a birthday cake or lighting the room on a dark night, the candle probably went out rather easily as long as you blew directly on the flame. But imagine "blowing out" a candle without actually blowing directly on the flame. It can be done. And it's not magic, just good science.

Question: Can you "blow out" a candle without blowing on the flame?

Materials
- Small votive candle
- Short drinking glass with a flat base
- Large drinking glass
- ½ cup vinegar
- Baking soda
- Spoon
- 3" x 5" note card
- Adult helper

Science Quote

"Nature and Nature's laws lay hid in night, God said: 'Let Newton be!,' and all was light."
—Alexander Pope, English poet

Procedure

1. Ask your helper to light the candle and carefully place it in the short glass so it sits flat on the bottom.
2. Pour one heaping spoonful of baking soda into the large glass.
3. Add the vinegar to the large glass. You should see a reaction almost immediately.
4. Hold the large glass over the small one with the note card placed over its top so the foam doesn't spill out.
5. Gently tip the large glass as if you were going to pour the vinegar into the smaller glass, but stop just as the liquid reaches the rim.
6. Watch what happens to the candle.

Poof!

To learn the answer to this silly science question, drop the letters into their proper place in the puzzle grid. The letters in each column fit in the spaces directly underneath that column, but in a different order! Black boxes are the spaces between the words.

If no one blew out the candles, which would burn longer — the candles on a boy's birthday cake, or the candles on a girl's birthday cake?

The Science Behind the Magic

It looks like the candle magically went out! You didn't blow on it, and in fact, it looks like nothing happened to it—it just went out on its own. But there's a science secret behind what's happening here. You see, when baking soda comes into contact with vinegar, a chemical reaction occurs. That's what causes the bubbles and foam you see. This reaction produces carbon dioxide, a gas you can't see or smell and the same gas you find in the bubbles in a can of soda. Carbon dioxide is heavier than air, which means it tends to fall down through the air toward the ground. What you did by "pouring" the large glass into the glass containing the candle was allow the carbon dioxide to escape from the reaction taking place in the large glass. It fell into the smaller glass, surrounded the candle, and caused it to go out.

Follow-Up

What's great about this experiment is that it is so easy to do over again. Go ahead and try it again! You might need to clean out the large glass and start with fresh vinegar, but each time you do, the results should be the same.

However, there is another way to blow out a candle without blowing directly on it. To do this, you need to place the lit candle flat on the table, and place a cylindrical object (such as a can of soda or a can of frozen juice concentrate) directly in front of the candle. All you need to do is blow toward the can—the can-

dle behind it should go out. How is this possible? The air isn't blocked by the can. Instead it splits, passes around it on either side, meets up again on the back side, and blows out the candle. Try this with different candles, and objects of different shapes in front. Why does a cylinder seem to be the shape for blowing out the hiding candle?

A cylinder has no edges to block or stop the air from flowing. Any other shape has at least one hard edge the air has to pass by, and hard edges disrupt the flow of air. But a cylinder tends to do the best job of allowing air to pass around it without disrupting its flow. Come to think of it, maybe that's why airplanes are the shape they are!

Did You Know?

- **Most of the air you breathe out is carbon dioxide.**

- **Carbon dioxide in its solid state is called** *dry ice*. **At room temperature, it changes from a solid directly to a gas though a process called** *sublimation*. **This gas appears as a fog and is commonly used in Halloween decorations.**

- **The average tree in a backyard removes 330 pounds of carbon dioxide from the air each year, while producing 260 pounds of oxygen.**

Burning at Both Ends

Question: Can you make a seesaw out of a candle?

Experiment Overview

Most people, when asked to imagine a see-saw, conjure up images of a playground with children sitting on either end of a large toy, bounding up and down, squealing with joy. For most people, and perhaps for you, this is their only experience with a seesaw. But in this experiment, you will be building your own seesaw, one that needs no outside help to keep rocking back and forth, can fit on your kitchen table, and is definitely not something children should be riding.

Science Concept

When a candle burns, it loses some of its wax, which melts and sometimes drips over the side. This can produce a big mess if it goes unnoticed, but in this case, that dripping is exactly what you want to see happen. You'll have to trim the bottom end of the candle, so that there is a wick on either end. Then, after you set up your balanced seesaw and light each end, the candle should rock back and forth as long as there is wax left to burn.

Materials
- Long (10-inch) taper candle
- Kitchen knife (to be used only by an adult)
- Ruler
- 2 straight pins
- 2 identical drinking glasses
- 2 small saucers
- Matches
- Adult partner

Procedure

1. Ask your adult partner cut about ½ to 1 inch off the bottom of the candle so that the wick is visible. It should stick out of the bottom just like it does the top.
2. Using the ruler, find the center of the candle and push one pin into each side of the candle at that point.
3. Carefully rest the pins on each glass so that the candle balances. It might take a few tries to get it just right. It should rock back and forth slowly.
4. Place one saucer under each end of the candle.
5. Light one end of the candle and let it burn until it starts to drip. When it does, light the other end and watch the candle begin to rock back and forth. You are truly "burning the candle at both ends."

Science Quote

"The universe is full of magical things, patiently waiting for our wits to grow sharper."

—Eden Philpotts, English science-fiction writer

Questions for the Scientist

1. Why might it be important to light the ends of the candle one at a time instead of at the same time?

_____

_____

_____

2. Imagine that you could place the candle high enough above the table that it would not touch the table if it tipped. How might the experiment change?

_____

_____

_____

3. How might your results change if the candle were not uniform in shape, that is, thicker on one end, thinner on the other?

_____

_____

_____

Science Fair: More Bounce to the Ounce

As you have probably noticed, some balls bounce better than others. For example, a football doesn't bounce all that high, but a golf ball will often bounce several times before coming to rest. These balls bounce the way they do because of what they are made of. But if you were to put some of the balls together, you would be amazed by the results.

Question: Which balls bounce best?

Experiment Overview

In this experiment, you will begin by dropping several balls of your choice, one at a time, from a predetermined height. You will measure their bounce height and record it in a data table. Then you will begin placing one ball on top of another and repeating the drops. This time, the heights to which the top ball bounces may surprise you. Your goal will be to determine which combination of balls produces the most impressive bounce of all.

Science Concept

When you drop a ball on the ground, some of its kinetic energy is transferred into the ground. The energy that remains is what makes the ball bounce back into the air. Some balls, such as golf balls and the super bouncy balls, retain most of the energy and bounce back to almost the same height from which

they were dropped. However, other balls, such as bowling balls (which should never be dropped on the ground), lose almost all of their energy and if they do bounce back up, don't go very high in the air.

However, when you place one ball on top of another, some of the bottom ball's energy is transferred into the top ball after the bounce, which can make the top ball appear to fly into the air. The heavier the bottom ball is compared to the top ball, the greater the effect.

Did You Know?

The term that describes how high a ball bounces when dropped is *coefficient of restitution*. It is found by comparing the bounce height to the drop height and taking the square root of the result.

Materials

- **Several round balls. Some possibilities are:**
    - **Basketball**
    - **Tennis ball**
    - **Rubber bouncy ball**
    - **Playground ball**
    - **Golf ball**
    - **Baseball**
- **Measuring tape**
- **Helper**
- **Open space for testing**

Procedure

1. Identify at least three balls you would like to use in the experiment.
2. Hold your arms straight out in front of you and have your helper measure their height above the ground. This will be the drop height for each of your trials.
3. With your helper ready to measure the bounce height, drop each ball by holding your arms directly in front of you and letting go of the ball.
4. Record the height to which each ball bounces.
5. Choose different pairings of balls to test. For example, you might select a tennis ball on top of a basketball.
6. Carefully hold the two balls at the same height as before with the one you chose to be on top sitting squarely on top of the bottom ball.
7. Drop the balls and have your helper measure the bounce height of the top ball. To double check, repeat this step until you feel confident in your measurement.
8. Repeat steps 5–7 as many times as you like. Be sure to try heavier balls on top of lighter balls as well.

Questions for the Scientist

1. Was there a difference in the results between placing a light ball on top of a heavy ball and placing a heavy ball on top of a light ball? Why do you think this difference exists?

   _____

   _____

2. In looking at your results, which factor do you think has the biggest impact on the bounce height: the weight of the ball or the material the ball is made of?

   _____

   _____

3. Do you think it's important that the balls be round? What might happen if you were to use a ball with a different shape?

   _____

   _____

4. Can you think of any applications for this idea that you could use in real life?

   _____

   _____

Conclusion

Your choice of balls and the order in which you placed them were both important decisions. Larger balls tend to have more energy, but they also weigh more. However, when their large energy is transferred to a much lighter ball, that energy goes a long way in making the smaller ball bounce. Can you imagine the effect if you were to try this experiment with three balls? What about four or more? It might be hard to keep them all balanced, but imagine the show you could put on!

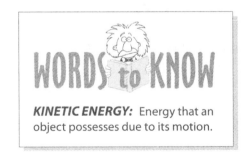

WORDS to KNOW

KINETIC ENERGY: Energy that an object possesses due to its motion.

Chapter 4

Water, Water, Everywhere

Did you know that approximately 70 percent of Earth's surface is covered in water? And yet, less than one-tenth of one percent of all that water is drinkable. In fact, if you were to fill a gallon jug of water, and thought of that gallon as being all the world's water, less than one teaspoon of that water would be drinkable. Water is a precious commodity in our world, and it also provides a great starting place for seeing some amazing science take place.

How much of the Earth's surface is covered with water?

In this chapter, you will get to explore the mysterious nature of water, and see some of its magical characteristics. You'll float paper clips, conjure up a magical water genie, make water disappear, and watch water change color.

Try This: The Amazing Leaking Bottle

There's nothing worse than opening up a bottle of water, starting to drink, and finding a hole in the side that has caused the water to spill out onto your face and shirt. Luckily, most water bottles, though made of plastic, don't have holes in them, so you can enjoy the water inside without worry about a leak. However, in this experiment you'll see how you can actually poke holes in a plastic container without the water spilling out.

Question: When does a hole not leak?

Materials
- **Plastic bag, preferably the kind found in produce sections at the grocery store**
- **Sharpened pencil**
- **Rubber band or twist-tie**
- **Water**
- **Shallow baking pan**

Procedure
1. To begin, fill the plastic bag with water until it is at least half full. Make sure there are no holes in the bag.
2. Tie off the top of the bag so there is still some air left between the water and the top of the bag.

Where Is the Water?

Use the directions to cross words out of the grid. When you are finished, read the remaining words from top to bottom and left to right. As if by magic, you will find the answer to this silly science riddle!

Cross out all the...
...two-letter words without N
...5th, 9th, and 15th letters
...words that rhyme with HOP

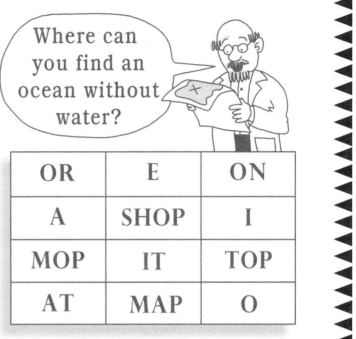

Where can you find an ocean without water?

OR	E	ON
A	SHOP	I
MOP	IT	TOP
AT	MAP	O

3. Carefully poke the pencil through the bag so it goes in one side of the bag and out the other.
4. Set the bag in the pan and look for any leaks.

The Science Behind the Magic

This experiment demonstrates as much about the properties of plastic as it does about water. You see, plastic is made from polymers, which are molecules that are chained together. These polymers give plastic its strength. In the case of plastic bags from the produce department, the polymers that are used actually shrink when cut. As a result, when you poked the pencil through the side of the bag, the plastic molecules shrank, and acted as a seal around the pencil. This is what kept the water from leaking.

Follow-Up

Can you think of a place where this sort of behavior could be useful? Where might someone want to have a material that reacts to a puncture by closing down and forming a seal?

One place this technology is being used is in automobile tires. Some new tires react to a puncture by forming an automatic seal over the hole. In some cases this is done by releasing a filler material inside the tire, but in others, the material shrinks and seals the hole, at least until the tire is made out of simply shrinks and seals the hole, at least until the owner can get to a repair shop.

Try This: Floating Metal

Question: Does metal float?

Materials
- **A cup of tap water**
- **Paper clips**
- **Liquid dish soap or a bar of soap**

Procedure
1. Bend one paper clip into a flat hook shape, so a second paper clip can be placed on the flat surface.
2. Try to place a paper clip on the surface of the water so that it does not sink.
3. Carefully place a second paper clip on the flat part of the unfolded paper clip and slowly lower it into the water. The paper clip should float.
4. Place a few drops of soap in the water, or touch the bar of soap to the water's surface and watch what happens to the paper clip.

The Science Behind the Magic
The paper clip floats because of the surface tension of the water. If you were to place the paper clip in the water at an angle or drop it from a height, the force would break the surface tension and it would sink. But gently lowering the paper clip onto the water allows the surface tension to stay intact and the paper clip floats. Adding the soap breaks the tension and the paper clip sinks to the bottom of the glass.

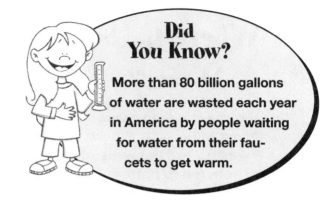

Did You Know?

More than 80 billion gallons of water are wasted each year in America by people waiting for water from their faucets to get warm.

Science Quote

"Water is H_2O, hydrogen two parts, oxygen one, but there is also a third thing, that makes it water and nobody knows what that is."
—D. H. Lawrence, British novelist

Water, Water, Everywhere

Follow-Up

You can extend this experiment by testing different objects, such as a needle or a small nail to see which ones float and which do not. Try to find out what shapes, sizes, and weights seem to work the best. Does soap always cause these other items to sink?

WORDS to KNOW

SURFACE TENSION: A result of water molecules squeezing together to produce a sort of lid on the surface of the water.

Did You Know?

It's true—metal does float! Large ships are often made out of steel or other kinds of metal and they float due to their shape. If a ship's metal was made into a ball of metal, it would sink, but because of its shape, it easily floats in water.

Abracadabra

Is it magic? Is it science? Or is it just silly?! To find the answer to this riddle, use a bright colored marker to highlight all the letters in the puzzle grid. Ignore the symbols, dollar signs, etc. Read the letters from left to right, and top to bottom.

How can you make a rock float?

@$P&#&$U>@&#>>T$
&#&$#@&>>I#&$&T@&
$I&$#@@>N#&#>&$$#
#&>$>#A@&#>#&>$>#@&
G#&>L$>#@@A$#@&S$&S$
&@#&>W$>#I@@>$T$#&H
#&>$>#@@&#&@$#A&#>
##S@#C&O$@>>O#&P&$
&#O&>$>#@$>##&F@&#
I$C@E$&#C>$R&#E@A&M#
$A>@#&>$N&#D>#@@>
S&#O#&#$>#M@$&#E&@
R$O@O&T>&B&#E@E>&#R

51

Sinking Oranges

Question: What makes an orange float or sink in water?

Experiment Overview

When first exploring water, many children wear water wings, life jackets, or other aids to help them stay afloat. But what does a piece of fruit wear in the water if it wants to keep from sinking? In this experiment, you will place fruits in water with and without their peels and decide which peels help keep their fruits high and dry.

Science Concept

The Greek scientist Archimedes once famously shouted "Eureka—I've found it!" when he discovered the concept of buoyancy and ran through the streets of town announcing his discovery. Unfortunately, this realization came to him while he was bathing in his bathtub…wearing no clothes. What Archimedes figured out is that objects have to move water out of the way in order to be placed in it. That water has weight. He found that the weight of that displaced water is the same as the force that lifts up the object in the water. If that force is enough, the object can float. A block of wood is an example of something that experiences a buoyant force equal to its weight. A bowling ball, however, doesn't experience a large enough buoyant force, and so it sinks.

Materials
- **Several pieces of fruit**
- **Large bowl of water**
- **Adult helper**
- **Knife, for peeling the fruit**

Procedure
1. Select a fruit and predict whether or not it will float when placed in the water.
2. Place the fruit in the water and observe whether or not it floats.
3. Ask your adult helper to assist you as you peel the fruit.

4. Once you have completely removed the peel, place the fruit in the water again and observe whether or not it floats.

5. Select another fruit and repeat steps 2–4. Do this for each fruit that you have selected for the experiment.

Questions for the Scientist

1. Which fruits floated when they still had their peels?

   _____

2. For the fruits that floated with their peels, what about their peels made them float?

   _____

3. Which fruits floated even without their peels?

   _____

4. Was there something those floating fruits had in common that made them float, even without their peels?

   _____

5. Using what you observed in this experiment, describe an outfit you could wear that would help keep you afloat in a swimming pool.

   _____

   _____

Follow-Up

Oranges tend to produce very specific results in experiments such as this one. That is because of the way their peels are made. On the surface of orange peels are hundreds of tiny pits that collect air. Collectively, these air pockets act like a sort of life preserver for the orange, and keep it afloat. When the peel is removed, the inside of the orange is heavier than the water, and it sinks to the bottom of the bowl. Other fruits that do not have these pits in their peels tend not to float as well as the oranges do. As a follow-up experiment, try other liquids such as salt water (which tends to be more dense than fresh water) or fruit juice to see if the same fruits produce the same results in these other liquids.

Science Online

Hurricanes form where winds and warm water meet. See how they work, learn about the devastation they can bring, and explore some fun hurricane activities at *http://42explore.com/ hurricane.htm*.

Try This: Water Genie

Question: Does Colored Water Rise?

Materials
- 2 identical small-mouthed bottles
- Food coloring
- Cold water
- Hot water
- 3" x 5" note card

Procedure
1. Fill one bottle with cold water.
2. Fill the other bottle with hot water from the tap.
3. Add food coloring to the hot water until its color is dark.
4. Place the note card over the top of the bottle containing the cold water.
5. Invert the bottle of cold water and place its mouth directly on top of the bottle containing the colored hot water.
6. Carefully remove the note card from between the two bottles.

The Science Behind the Magic
When you remove the note card, you should begin to see wisps of colored water rising into the upper bottle. It's not a magic water genie. Instead, it's the hot water trading places with the cold water. You see, hot water is less dense than cold water. So when the two are placed together, the cold water falls to the bottom while the hot water rises. If all the water were clear, you might not see this exchange happen. But because you colored the hot water, you can see it rise, even while the cold water falls into the lower bottle.

Follow-Up
Water is not the only substance that behaves in this way. You may have noticed in the summer that the upper floors of your house tend to be warmer and the lower floors tend to be cooler. This is because, like water, hot air is less dense than cold air, so it rises to the top of the building. If you have a ceiling fan in your house, check to see if it has a direction switch on it. Those that do are designed to circulate cool air up from the ground during hot weather, and warm air down from the ceiling during cool weather.

Try This:
Disappearing Water

Every house with small children living in it has at one time or another experienced the unfortunate results of a spilled glass of water, juice, or milk. It happens, and while it's usually quickly cleaned up, it's not typically one of the happiest activities for a parent. But just imagine if there were something a parent could use that would make a spilled drink completely disappear. Imagine further that this magic material were already in the homes of many families with small children. Wouldn't that be something?

Dizzy Drops

Strings of molecules bond together to form plastic, but in this puzzle strings of letters bond together to give you the silly answer to a riddle! Use the clues to fill in the drops. The last letter of one word is the first letter of the next! HINT: Fill the drops in order, even though it sometimes looks as if you are spelling backward.

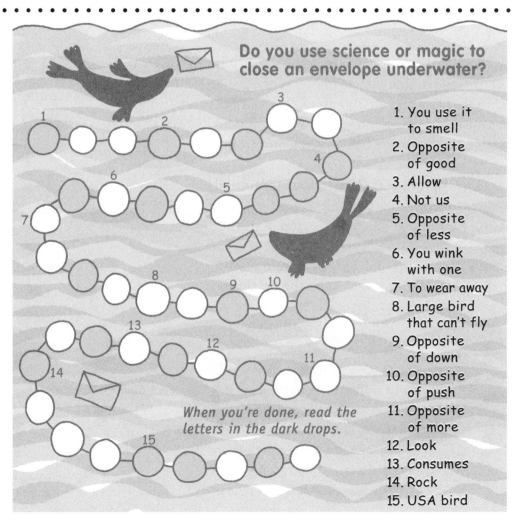

Do you use science or magic to close an envelope underwater?

1. You use it to smell
2. Opposite of good
3. Allow
4. Not us
5. Opposite of less
6. You wink with one
7. To wear away
8. Large bird that can't fly
9. Opposite of down
10. Opposite of push
11. Opposite of more
12. Look
13. Consumes
14. Rock
15. USA bird

When you're done, read the letters in the dark drops.

Question: Can you make water disappear?

Materials
- **A few disposable diapers**
- **Water**
- **Measuring cups**

Procedure
1. Open a disposable diaper and lay it flat on a table.
2. Pour one cup of water into the thick part of the diaper and watch what happens.
3. Repeat step 2 until no more water can be absorbed. Keep track of how many cups of water the diaper held.

The Science Behind the Magic
The water doesn't actually disappear, of course. It's absorbed by the material in the diaper. This material is another kind of polymer, called sodium polyacrylate, particles of which are about the size of regular table salt when dry. When the particles get wet, however, they absorb water until they swell to nearly four times their original size. What's more, these particles don't stick together, but remain separate. This provides extra comfort for babies with wet diapers and offers you an interesting extension activity.

Follow-Up
Take another diaper and with an adult's help, cut it open so you can see the materials inside. Pour these materials into an empty cup, preferably a clear one. Now slowly pour water into the cup and watch how the particles

Did You Know?
The first disposable diaper can be traced back to the year 1950. Today, nearly 20 billion disposable diapers are used each year in the United States.

Science Online

Visit the HowStuffWorks. com Web site to learn more about the magic behind disposable diapers: *http:// science.howstuffworks.com/ question207.htm.*

absorb water and grow. Keep pouring water into the cup until all the dry particles are wet. Can you turn the cup upside down without any water falling out? Depending on how much water you poured and how much of the absorbent diaper material you used, you may find that nothing comes out at all. Then, try adding some table salt and mixing with a spoon. You should see the water come back, as the salt reacts with the gel you produced to release the water.

Science Fair: Changing Water Colors

Have you ever tried to mix several colors together to make new colors, only to find that you ended up with a dark brown or black mixture? This typically happens when you mix multiple colors together. But sometimes, if you mix the right colors in the right order, you can produce a surprising result that will amaze you.

Question: Can you mix colors to end up with your original color?

Experiment Overview

If you were to mix several paint colors together, you would undoubtedly produce a black or very dark brown color. But in this experiment, it's the order in which you mix the colors, combined with the types of liquid you are mixing, that makes the experiment work. Instead of using colored water, you will use grape juice, ammonia, and vinegar. The reactions, completed in the correct order, will produce color changes that end up giving you the same color of liquid that you begin with.

SAFETY NOTE: Do not drink any of the liquids in this experiment. They may look safe, but can be very dangerous.

WORDS to KNOW

INDICATOR: A liquid that changes color in the presence of an acid or a base.

BASE: Chemical opposite of an acid. Bases tend to be bitter tasting as opposed to sour-tasting acids. Bases in large concentrations can be very dangerous.

Science Concept

The key to this experiment is the use of grape juice. Grape juice is an indicator that can tell you whether an acid or base is present. Depending on what kind of liquid you mix it with, it will change colors. When an indicator mixes with a base, it tends to turn green, and when it mixes with an acid, it tends to turn red. The key is trying to understand which of the other liquids is an acid and which is a base.

Materials

- **3 small drinking glasses**
- **Unsweetened grape juice**
- **Water**
- **Liquid ammonia**
- **Vinegar**
- **Measuring spoons**
- **Eyedropper**

Procedure

1. Mix one tablespoon of unsweetened grape juice with about four ounces of water in one of the three glasses. It should have a pale reddish color.
2. Place 5–7 drops of ammonia in the second glass.
3. Place 10–15 drops of vinegar in the third glass.
4. Carefully pour the grape juice from the first glass into the second and gently swirl until it is completely mixed. Make a note of the color of the new liquid mixture.
5. Finally, pour the liquid from the second glass into the third and swirl until it is completely mixed. Make a note of the color of the new liquid.

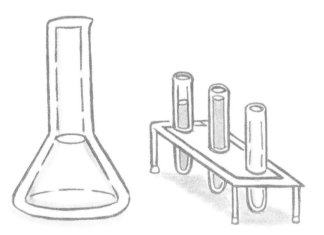

Water, Water, Everywhere

Questions for the Scientist

1. Describe the colors of your liquids in each stage of the experiment.

   _____

   _____

2. Based on the description given at the beginning of the experiment, do you think that ammonia is an acid or a base?

   _____

   _____

3. Based on the descriptions given at the beginning of the experiment, do you think that vinegar is an acid or a base?

   _____

   _____

4. What do you think would have happened if you had mixed the liquids in a different order? Try it and see what happens.

   _____

   _____

Did You Know?

Baking soda, a leavening agent, helps cookies rise as they bake, and can also be used to clean up after the cookies are done baking.

Conclusion

When indicators, such as diluted grape juice, mix with acids, they tend to turn a reddish color, but when they mix with bases, they tend to turn blue or green. Mixing the liquids in the order you did allowed the grape juice to change first to a greenish color, and then back to a reddish color. Some fruits, such as lemons and oranges, contain an acid called citric acid, while other acids, such as vinegar, are commonly used in cooking. Bases such as ammonia are often used as cleaners and should be avoided by children. However, other bases, such as baking soda, are used to make cakes and cookies or to keep refrigerators smelling fresh. Remember that if you aren't sure what something is, you should never put it in your mouth to test it. Ask an adult what it is, or to help you set up a test with an acid-base indicator.

Most people are aware of the amazing things the human body can do. Feats of strength, the ability for a cut or broken bone to heal itself, and the magic that turns energy in the food you eat into the energy you need to run, jump, and live. What you might not be as aware of, however, is that your body has some pretty interesting scientific abilities. These skills allow you to use your five senses to interact with the world around you in exciting and sometimes unexpected ways.

In this chapter, you will explore the human body and some of the ways it is different from the body of any other animal on the planet. You will turn your fingers into sausages, discover your magical voice, and put math and music together to produce magical sounds.

Did You Know?

The human mouth has around 10,000 taste buds, but they are not all on the tongue. Some are under the tongue, some are on the cheeks, and some on the lips.

Try This: Acquiring a Taste

Question: Can you fool your taste buds?

Materials
- **Blindfold**
- **Peanut butter, vanilla extract, or cinnamon**
- **A variety of foods, cut up into small pieces. Some possibilities are:**
  - **-Apple   -Carrot**
  - **-Potato   -Meat, such as ham,**
  - **-Onion   turkey, chicken, beef, or**
  - **-Pear   steak**

Procedure
1. Cut up the foods you wish to test into small, bite-sized pieces.
2. Arrange the foods on a plate.
3. Rub either the peanut butter, vanilla, or cinnamon on your upper lip.
4. Cover your eyes with the blindfold.
5. Place each of the food items in your mouth, one at a time, and try to determine which food it is.
6. If you have some friends handy, recruit one or more of them to try their hand at identifying the foods with one of the distractor foods on their upper lip.

The Science Behind the Magic

When you eat food, the taste buds on your tongue detect certain types of flavors. There are regions of your tongue that sense sweet tastes, such as sugary foods; sour tastes, such as lemon juice; salty tastes, such as potato chips; and bitter tastes, such as ground coffee. But there is more to tasting food than simply relying on your taste buds. Think back to the last time you had a severe cold. Chances are, your ability to taste food when your cold was at its worst was affected. You see, your nose also plays a role in tasting food. When you plug your nose, your brain is not able to process the tastes that come from your taste buds as well as when your nose is clear. So some foods with similar textures, such as apples and raw potatoes, will seem to taste the same when you plug your nose. But even with your nose unplugged, your ability to identify foods can be reduced by introducing strong alternate flavors, such as cinnamon or vanilla, around

your mouth. These strong flavors drown out the flavors of the foods you are eating.

Another key part of tasting foods is what you see with your eyes. For example, when you pick up a piece of chocolate and put it in your mouth you know what you expect as far as its taste. But if you cover your eyes so you can't see what you are eating, the expectation of what it will taste like is gone, and it becomes more difficult to tell what you are eating.

Follow-Up

Think about the types of foods that were easier to identify than others. What sort of characteristics do these foods have in common? Do you think certain people are better at tasting certain foods than others? If you are up for some research, look into the world of "supertasters." These people tend to respond to certain flavors, bitter in particular, in intense ways, making it very difficult for them to enjoy foods with those flavors.

Science Online

Want to learn how animals taste and use their other senses? To learn lots of interesting animal sense facts, visit: *www.indianchild .com/what_do_animals_see.htm.*

Taste the Difference

These scientists are eating lunch, but something is not right with the food! Use the words scattered around the page to fill in the blanks, and complete each scientist's complaint. The trick is to make the adjective and the food go together! (See the sample, right.)

"Please pass the <u>sugar</u>!" Lee said <u>sweetly</u>.

BITTERLY

HOTLY

CHILI

LEMON

PICKLES

SOURLY

ICILY

PEPPERS

SHERBET

"This _____ tastes awful!" Beth said _____.

"I can't eat the _____ _____!" Pam said _____.

"The _____ is too cold!" Jan said _____.

"I don't like the _____!" Ron said _____.

Try This: Blue, Black, and Yellow Patriotism

Question: Can you draw a U.S. flag with yellow, black, and green markers?

Materials

- 3" x 5" lined note card
- Yellow, black, and green markers
- Blank sheet of white computer paper

Procedure

1. Place the note card so that its longer side lies horizontally.
2. In the upper left corner of the note card, draw a rectangle that is 2 inches wide and about 1½ inches tall.
3. Draw a horizontal line through the middle of the white space at the top of the card to produce thirteen lines on the card.
4. Color 50 stars (or as many as you can fit) in the rectangular area you marked off with the black marker. Fill in the rest of the rectangle with yellow.
5. Alternating black and green, fill in each line on the rest of the card.
6. Stare at the drawing on the note card for at least 30 seconds.
7. Look immediately at the blank sheet of computer paper until you see an image of the flag appear.

Science Quote

"The purpose of life, after all, is to live it, to taste experience to the utmost, to reach out eagerly and without fear for newer and richer experiences."
—Eleanor Roosevelt, former first lady

Did You Know?

The rainbow patterns you can see when oil (or gasoline) floats on water are caused by light reflecting through different thicknesses of the oil. This is known as "thin-film interference." This also happens when you blow bubbles and look at them on a sunny day.

Something Is Fishy

This scientist has been experimenting with a piano and a fish. What did she discover? Use the note decoder to find out!

The Incredible Machine

The Science Behind the Magic

Your are able to see when your eyes respond to light rays that enter them. However, intense concentration on a certain color of light causes your eyes to tire. As a result, when you look away from that color, your eyes will see the opposite of that color in what is called an *afterimage*. In this activity, you tired your eyes out by staring at the green, black, and yellow colors. When you looked away at the white page, your eyes showed you the opposite colors in the flag, which are red, white, and blue.

Follow-Up

See if you can come up with other afterimage drawings and show them to your friends. Experiment with different colors to see how realistic you can make your afterimages look.

Blowing Blue

Use a blue marker to color all the shapes containing the letters P-U-F-F. As if by magic, you will find the silly answer to this riddle!

Drew was the winner of a five-mile race, but he was a loser at the same time. What did Drew lose?

Stomach Acid

Question: Which antacid works best when you have an upset stomach?

Experiment Overview

Each time you eat something, your stomach produces acid, which helps your body digest the food. Too much acid can cause indigestion, or an upset stomach. In this experiment, you will test different antacids to see which of them neutralize acid the best. You will use an acid-base indicator, made from red cabbage, to test the success of the antacids.

Science Concept

In your stomach, acid is used to break down the food you eat so that it can be digested and converted to energy for your body. However, sometimes your stomach produces too much acid, and it causes a feeling of discomfort. In addition, that acid can sometimes come up your throat, giving you a burning feeling in your chest commonly known as heartburn. To counteract this acid buildup, people usually take antacids, which are tablets containing ingredients that neutralize the acidity in their stomach. You will be using carbonated soda to simulate the acid in your stomach and will use the red cabbage indicator to test to see how well each antacid works.

The redder the indicator is, the more acidic the material you are testing. As more of the acid is neutralized, the indicator turns first a bluish, and then a greenish color.

Materials

- 1 (2-liter) bottle of carbonated soda
- Several short drinking glasses
- Several brands of antacid, available for purchase in a drugstore
- Baking soda
- Spoon
- Jar of canned red cabbage, available for purchase in a grocery store
- Several small saucers, such as those you would use with coffee cups

Procedure

1. Drain the juice from the jar of red cabbage. This will serve as your acid indicator.
2. Pour a small amount of the indicator into each saucer.
3. Pour the soda into each of the drinking glasses.

4. Gently crumble one tablet of each of the antacids you are testing into the drinking glasses containing carbonated soda.
5. Add one spoonful of baking soda to its own glass of soda.
6. Use the spoon to stir each antacid into the soda until it is completely dissolved. Rinse the spoon after stirring in each glass.
7. Add one spoonful of each soda mixture to its own saucer of acid indicator and stir gently to mix. Be sure to rinse the spoon after each mixture.
8. Observe the final color of the acid indicator and determine which antacid was most effective at neutralizing the acid in the soda.

Questions for the Scientist

1. Which of the antacids was the best at neutralizing the acid in the soda?

_____

2. Which foods do you think are most likely to produce heartburn or discomfort in your stomach?

_____

3. Are all acids dangerous for you? Research foods that contain acid to see which are healthy and which are not.

_____

Follow-Up

Your stomach is an incredible machine. It takes all the food you eat and converts it into the energy you need in order to run, play, laugh, learn, and live. Take care of it and it will last you a lifetime. That means eating well, keeping yourself active, and living a healthy lifestyle.

Try This: Magical Hands

Question: Can you fool your eyes into thinking they are seeing something that isn't there?

Materials
- Your hands
- Small tube

Procedure
1. Stick your index fingers out, facing one another, in front of your face.
2. Allow your eyes to relax as you focus your attention on an object far off in the distance.
3. Slowly move your fingers toward one another until a small "sausage" appears between them.

The Science Behind the Magic

Human vision is called *binocular,* which means you see with two eyes. What happens is that each eye actually sees a slightly different picture. The combination of the two viewpoints allows us to tell when something lies in front of or behind something else. It's what allows us to see in three dimensions. In fact, if you were to close one eye and look around, you would only see in two dimensions. It's only by

See That?

Optical illusions are puzzles designed to fool your eyes and brain. These two are classics!

Do you see the white triangle? Look carefully — can you find the lines that make up its edges?

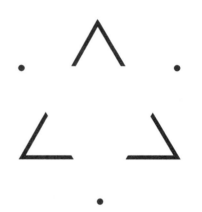

Do you see a flat shape with six sides, or a three dimensional transparent box? Try to go back and forth between the two.

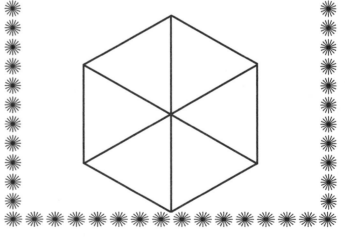

moving your head around, or opening your other eye that you can tell how far away objects are.

In this experiment, the "sausage" is actually just each of the tips of your fingers, viewed from each eye, overlapping one another. Try the experiment again and notice that outside the "sausage," you can see images of your fingers. Each one, however, is being seen from different eyes. When those images overlap, it appears to form a small sausage-like shape of your fingers. Your eyes are fooled into thinking they are seeing something they are not actually seeing.

Follow-Up

Another fun "trick" to play on your eyes involves holding a small tube in front of one of your eyes. Roll a sheet of computer paper into a tube that is 11 inches long and about ½ inch in diameter. Tape the paper so your tube keeps its shape. With both eyes open, hold the tube up to one eye and look through it. Hold your other hand next to the tube, about two-thirds of the way down the tube. Since one eye will be seeing through the tube to what lies beyond, and the other will be seeing your hand, the two images overlap to make it appear that there is a hole in your hand. This is another example of the effects of binocular vision. See if you can use your binocular vision to come up with new ways to fool your eyes.

BINOCULAR VISION: Being able to see with both eyes, each from a slightly different angle, which allows you to see in three dimensions.

Science Online

At this site, you can see optical illusions organized by type. Learn more about how eyes can be fooled at: *www.colorcube.com /illusions/illusion.htm.*

Magic Breath

Question: Can your breath clean water?

Experiment Overview

In this experiment you will take a bottle of water that has been colored red and, simply by talking into it, change the coloring of the water. You will first have to use the proper form of coloring, as only certain liquids will react to your voice in this way. Then, it simply takes patience, and having a lot to say, before you can see the results of this amazing process.

Science Concept

Phenol red is a special form of dye often found in pool supply stores or drugstores. When added to the water in a pool, it changes color based on the acidity of the water. The change that occurs in the test water tells the tester whether the pool is safe for swimming, or whether additional chemicals should be added before anyone enters. This experiment reverses the process. The phenol red turns the water a light red color. By talking into the bottle, you are breathing out carbon dioxide, which reacts with the water to produce a weak acid. Slowly, as more carbon dioxide is breathed out, the acid that forms changes the red color in the water. In time, the red color will be a different color.

SAFETY NOTE: It is not safe to drink water that has been mixed with chemicals, no matter how clean it appears. Be sure to discard any water you use in a science experiment, and to only drink water that you know to be clean and safe.

Materials

- 1 small bottle of phenol red
- Baking soda
- Empty 500-mL (about 16-ounces) wide-mouth bottle with screw-on cap
- Tap water

Procedure

1. Fill the bottle with approximately 250 mL (8 ounces) of tap water.
2. Add three drops of phenol red to the water, screw on the cap, and swirl the bottle to mix the color.
3. If you don't see the water change color noticeably, try adding small amounts of baking soda and swirling. Baking soda should bring out the red color in the water.

4. Unscrew the cap and speak into the bottle. You might try saying one sentence at a time.
5. Replace the lid and swirl the bottle.
6. Repeat steps 4 and 5 until you begin to see the color in the bottle change.
7. If you wish to repeat this experiment, simply add more baking soda to the water mixture until the water turns a red color again.

Questions for the Scientist

1. How long did it take until the red color began to change in the bottle?

   _____
   _____
   _____

2. Do you think that the same sort of reaction would happen if you left the water out in the open for a period of time? Why or why not?

   _____
   _____
   _____

3. What sorts of materials could you add to a phenol-red water solution that might produce the same effects as those you found in this experiment? You might want to ask a parent for help with this question.

   _____
   _____
   _____

4. Do you think it would be possible to use people's breath to clean a swimming pool? Why or why not?

   _____
   _____
   _____

Science Fair: Making Magical Music

More than two thousand years ago, one of the greatest mathematicians of all time, Pythagoras, discovered a connection between math and music that young musicians have been putting to use ever since. He figured out that two musical notes played on strings with the correct lengths produced notes that sounded nice together. Others sounded really bad. Now you get to explore this amazing relationship.

Question: Which musical notes sound good together?

Experiment Overview

You will be using a list of frequencies and a piano to produce pairs of tones. You will then ask several of your friends or family members to tell you which pairs sound good together, and which ones produce sounds that don't go together. After you survey your test subjects, you will then put together a prediction as to the pairings that produce the most pleasant sounds.

Science Concept

Pythagoras discovered that certain frequencies of musical notes seemed to match better with others. In his day, he could produce these notes by plucking strings of different lengths. Today, we have pianos that can produce the different notes. When two notes with frequencies in specific ratios, such as 2:1, 3:2, 4:3, etc., are played together, the resulting sound is generally a pleasant one to hear. However, other ratios often produce sounds that do not sound good together. This is due to the patterns of the sound waves and how they interfere with one another. When the patterns interfere in a regular pattern, the notes sound nice together. When they do not interfere in this manner, they do not sound nice together.

The Incredible Machine

Materials

- **Piano or similar keyboard**
- **Chart of musical frequencies**
- **Test subjects**

Procedure

1. Use the included list of pairs and play each pair in order for your test subject.

C-D	D-F	E-B
C-E	D-G	F-G
C-F	D-A	F-A
C-G	D-B	F-B
C-A	E-F	G-A
C-B	E-G	G-B
D-E	E-A	A-B

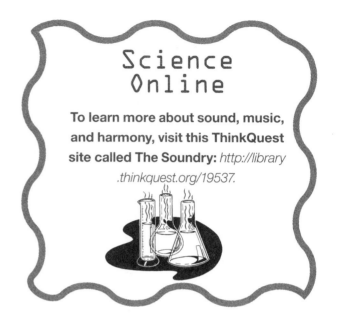

Science Online

To learn more about sound, music, and harmony, visit this ThinkQuest site called **The Soundry:** *http://library .thinkquest.org/19537.*

2. For each pair, have your test subject decide whether or not the combination makes a pleasant sound or an unpleasant one.
3. Repeat steps 1 and 2 for each of your test subjects.
4. Use your data to compile a list of those note pairs that your subjects enjoyed hearing and those pairings that they did not enjoy.
5. Compare the frequency ratios of the pairs your subjects chose to those listed to determine if they found the same ratios as Pythagoras did.

WORDS to KNOW

CHORD: A combination of three or more musical notes that make a pleasant sound.

FREQUENCY: A count of the number of waves produced by a certain sound each second.

Questions for the Scientist

1. How accurately did your subjects' choices match the pairs that Pythagoras discovered?

   _____

   _____

   _____

2. Can you predict combinations of three or more notes that you think would sound good together? In music, these combinations are known as chords.

   _____

   _____

   _____

3. Notes on a piano are grouped into octaves. Do you think that if you chose a different octave, with its associated frequencies, the note pairings that sound nice together would stay the same? Why or why not?

   _____

   _____

   _____

Chapter 6

Bubble, Bubble, Toil and Trouble

Of all the sciences you may study in your lifetime, one stands out as most likely to produce results that will shock and amaze you. Chemistry has for years presented its observers with physical and chemical changes that often seem to be unexplainable. The magic of chemistry, however, can always be explained by science. Whether it's a change in form or shape, or a change in what the material is actually made out of, chemical reactions make for some real eye-opening experiences. In this chapter you will make plastic on the kitchen stove, change water's color with your own hand, make fog in a jar, and light a candle with no wick.

Did You Know?

The ocean has a salt content of around 3.5 percent.

Try This: Crystals in a Pan

If you've ever been to the ocean and had the chance to swim or play in salt water, you know that while it tastes different than fresh water, to look at it, you would be hard-pressed to see any noticeable differences. However, as you will see in this experiment, salt water is actually very different from fresh water.

Question: What sorts of things grow in salt water?

Materials
- **Black construction paper**
- **Pie plate**
- **Warm water**
- **Epsom salt**
- **Measuring cup**
- **Spoon**

Procedure
1. Cut out a circle of paper just large enough to fit in the bottom of the pie plate.
2. Add ¼ cup of Epsom salt to 1 cup of warm water and stir until the salt is completely dissolved.
3. Place the paper in the bottom of the pie plate.
4. Pour the salt water into the pie plate and place it in a sunny or warm location.
5. As the water evaporates, you should start to see salt crystals form.

Bubble, Bubble, Toil and Trouble

The Science Behind the Magic

When salt is dissolved in water, it forms crystals. The crystals form together into larger structures, but they are not visible when the water is present. When it evaporates, the crystals that were formed are left behind and become visible on the paper. It turns out that different kinds of salt produce crystals of different size and shape. In fact, each time you do this experiment, you will probably get a different set of crystals.

Follow-Up

If you wish to repeat this experiment, try using regular table salt or rock salt to see what sorts of new shapes you can produce. Also, you can try mixing food coloring into the water to see what sorts of colored crystals you can produce. Can you make a set of multicolored crystals? You can also adjust the temperature of the water to see if crystals form better at one temperature over another. You may also wish to adjust the temperature of the air during the evaporation process to see whether rapid evaporation in warm air produces better crystals than a slower evaporation in cooler air.

Science Online

Learn more about the water cycle at this Kid Zone site: *www.kidzone.ws/water.*

Try This: Hand of Magic

People are probably telling you all the time to wash your hands. Before you eat, you have to wash your hands. When you come inside after playing, you wash your hands. When you cough or sneeze, you wash your hands. But in this experiment, you will show that there is magic in your hands. And yes, you should still wash those hands after you finish, but only after making some magic of your own.

Question: is there magic in your hands?

Materials

- **Clear plastic container or mixing bowl**
- **Large clear glass or plastic pitcher**
- **Iodine**
- **Liquid starch, such as you would use when washing clothes**
- **Vitamin C in tablet form**
- **Spoon**

Procedure

1. Pour one cup of liquid starch into the bowl.
2. Fill the pitcher with water from the tap.
3. Put several drops of iodine into the pitcher and stir until the water turns a yellowish color.
4. Put one hand in the yellow-colored water and stir it around.
5. Put your other hand in the bowl with the liquid starch, so that your palm is covered.
6. Now place your starch-covered hand in the pitcher and watch as the water turns a dark blue.
7. Remove your hand from the water.
8. With your "clean" hand, pick up the Vitamin C tablet and hold it as you place your hand in the pitcher. As the vitamin tablet dissolves, you should see the water turn clear again.

The Science Behind the Magic

This really isn't magic either. Iodine is an indicator for starch (meaning that iodine solutions change color in the presence of starch). When you put your first hand in the iodine solution, there was no starch on it, so it didn't change color. However, when you placed your other hand, the hand that had been dipped in liquid starch, in the same solution, the iodine reacted to the starch and turned a dark blue color. The addition of vitamin C caused

WORDS to KNOW

STARCH: A complex carbohydrate that can be dissolved in water. Foods containing starch make up more than half of the average person's diet. The four main starchy foods are rice, potatoes, corn, and wheat.

the iodine solution to change slightly, just enough to remove the color from the water. This experiment can be repeated over and over again as long as there is still iodine in the water and you introduce more starch to the iodine solution.

Follow-Up

Starches are a big part of most people's diets. Foods such as corn, pasta, peas, beans, potatoes (including potato chips), and rice are common examples of starches that you may eat regularly. But other foods provide you with starches also. Foods such as artichokes and sweet potatoes, or yams, also are considered starches. You can test each of these food items for starch content by performing a similar test to the one described above. Simply prepare an iodine solution, or use a few drops of pure iodine, and place it on the food you wish to test. If the iodine, which is normally a yellowish color, turns a dark blue, then you have found a starch. You might be surprised at what you discover. Be sure NEVER to eat any food you have tested in a science experiment.

Safety First

You must be careful when doing experiments in chemistry. Break the "Vowel Switch" code to learn an important safety tip!

Tha mist empirtunt theng yio laurn en chamestry cluss es "Navar leck tha spiin!"

Plastic in a Pot

Question: How do you make plastic?

Experiment Overview

Yes, you read correctly—you can make your own plastic in your own kitchen, with ingredients most people already have on hand. It may require some adult help when working with the stove, but if you follow the steps carefully, you should be able to produce your very own ball of plastic. You'll be cooking up some milk and vinegar and separating the products at just the right time to produce your final product.

Science Concept

Most plastic made today began with chemicals called petrochemicals, which lie far beneath the surface of the earth where oil is found. Plastic-making is a complicated process that involves drilling, transporting, and refining oil, and then extracting the petrochemicals necessary to make the plastic. Lucky for you, you can make your own version of plastic by using simple household ingredients. It won't be as versatile as the plastic you see in stores, forming bottles, containers, parts for your car, etc., but it's a lot safer to make and you won't have to build an oil refinery to do it.

Materials

- **1 cup milk, 2% or whole milk**
- **¼ cup of vinegar**
- **Small pot or saucepan**
- **Old handkerchief or washcloth**
- **Adult helper**

PETROCHEMICAL: Chemicals made from oil found under the earth's surface that are used in making plastic.

Procedure

1. Heat the milk on the stove until just before it begins to boil.
2. Add the vinegar slowly and mix together.

3. The two ingredients should slowly separate into a thick white substance and a watery solution.
4. When these materials have separated, pour the contents of the saucepan through the handkerchief. Let the liquid run through the handkerchief. Squeeze out the remaining liquid.
5. Let your plastic ball sit for an hour while it hardens.

The Science Behind the Magic

Vinegar is an acid. It reacts with milk to produce rubbery clumps of casein, a protein in milk, and separate it from the rest of the liquid. After draining off the excess liquid, the solid clumps can be molded while still warm. Once cooled, the solid will set in its final shape as plastic. This method of producing plastic, while fairly simple, is not very cost-effective, which is why many plastics today are made from oil products and other commonly available materials. The problem is that soon we will run out of many of these materials, such as oil, and will have to look elsewhere for the ingredients to make plastic.

Questions for the Scientist

1. What do you think caused the milk to change into plastic?

_____

_____

2. What did the plastic you made look and feel like? Compare it to another plastic object in your house—was your plastic realistic?

_____

_____

3. Do you think this would be a practical way to make plastic? What might some problems be with using this process on a large scale?

_____

_____

Follow-Up

You can try this experiment again by changing one of the variables. Try using different types of milk, such as nonfat, chocolate, or dry milk, to see if the effects are the same. You can also try different kinds of vinegar to see which one produces the most realistic form of plastic. As a scientist, make sure you change only one variable at a time to see whether that change had the desired effect.

Important Ingredient

Color in the squares with horizontal lines to find the silly science answer!

What is the quickest way to make oil boil?

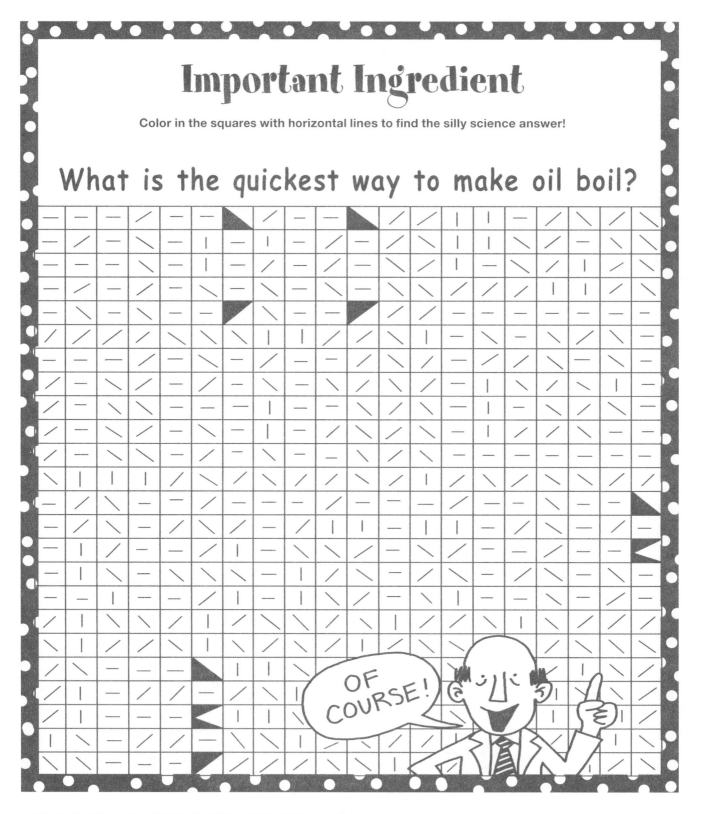

Try This: Fog Chamber

No matter where you live, you have probably experienced fog at some point in your life. Fog often forms overnight as air that is filled with moisture cools down to a point at which the moisture condenses on particles in the air, forming fog at ground level. In its simplest form, fog is just a cloud that is touching the earth. But you can produce your own fog in this simple experiment.

Question: How does fog form?

Materials
- **Large (1 gallon) glass or plastic jar with wide mouth**
- **1 surgical-type rubber glove**
- **Matches**
- **Water**
- **Adult helper**

Procedure

1. Pour just enough water into the jar to cover the bottom.
2. Turn the glove upside down, so its fingers are pointing down, and push it down into the jar. Stretch the glove's opening over the mouth of the jar to serve as a lid. The glove should be hanging, fingers down, into the jar.
3. This step will require an adult's help. Have your adult helper light a match. Carefully

Did You Know? Snow melts faster on a foggy day than when no fog is present.

pull part of the glove back from the rim so your adult helper can drop the lit match into the jar. Quickly replace the glove across the mouth to reseal the jar.

4. Now place your hand in the glove and pull upward. A cloud of fog should form and will stay present until you place the glove back into its original location.

The Science Behind the Magic

When you sealed the jar, you trapped liquid water, water vapor, and smoke inside the jar. When you pulled the glove outward, you caused things to change rather dramatically. For one, you caused the air inside the jar to expand, or fill up more space. That effectively cools the air to a point where the water vapor in the air condenses on particles in the air. When the air cools, the water molecules in the air slow down and stick to the smoke particles, forming tiny fog particles. When you push the glove back into the jar, however, the air warms back up, the water molecules turn back into liquid water, and the fog goes away.

Making Slime

Question: is slime a liquid or a solid?

Experiment Overview

In this experiment you will be making a substance that sometimes acts like a liquid and sometimes acts like a solid. It's really pretty easy to make and once you get done, you can play with it for hours. You can even add coloring to your slime and make a rainbow of colors to play with.

Science Concept

The combination of water and cornstarch, in just the right amounts, produces a substance called a *colloid*. This particular colloid has cornstarch particles spread evenly through the water. Left to itself, the mixture takes on the properties of the water, in that it tends to behave like a liquid. However, when someone touches it, the cornstarch particles compress together and form into a solid. When the pressure is released, the liquid behavior returns.

Materials

- ½ cup of cornstarch
- ¼ cup of warm water
- Mixing bowl
- Spoon
- Food coloring (optional)

Procedure

1. Pour the cornstarch into the bowl.
2. Slowly add the water, a little at a time until the mixture becomes slightly runny. As you mix, it may seem to have turned to a solid, but once you stop, it will appear runny again.
3. Add food coloring if you wish.
4. Pour the slime into your hand and begin experimenting with it. If the slime is still too runny, add a little more cornstarch. If it's still too thick, return it to the bowl and add a little water until it thins out.

Questions for the Scientist

1. What kind of solid did your slime feel like when you held it in your hand?

   _____

   _____

   _____

2. When it was in liquid form, what did your slime feel like?

   _____

   _____

   _____

3. What do you think will happen to your slime if you leave it out in the open air?

   _____

   _____

   _____

4. Colloids are fascinating substances. Can you think of any other colloids that you might have encountered in your life? If so, can you think of any way to separate the two materials once they are mixed?

   _____

   _____

   _____

Follow-Up

Once you have made slime, you might want to experiment with some other interesting materials that are similar. For example, you can make a putty that has a rubbery feel to it by combining one cup of white glue and one cup of liquid starch. You can color your putty by adding food coloring. You can also make a substitute Silly Putty material (great for stretching and for copying newsprint) by combining ½ cup of water, ½ cup of white glue, and ½ cup of a borax solution. The borax solution is made of one tablespoon of borax and ½ cup of water. Mix it all up and store in an airtight bag or container. After an hour or so, your putty should be ready.

Science Fair: Candle in the Wind

When you light a candle with a flame, you usually have to touch the flame to the candle's wick. The flame then ignites the wick and the wax surrounding the wick. As the wick slowly burns, it burns off the wax around it. The candle remains lit as long as there is wax to burn. Once the wax is all burned, the candle is done. When someone blows out a candle, there is usually a thin stream of smoke that continues to rise off the wick even after the flame dies. This thin stream of smoke is going to be the critical piece to this experiment.

Question: Can you relight a candle without touching the wick?

Experiment Overview

For this experiment you will need to assemble a variety of sizes and shapes of candles. Using the same equipment, you'll be lighting the candles, blowing them out, and then trying to relight them in the smoke rising from the wick. You will want to test to see just how far above the wick you can place the lighted match in order to relight the candle. You may also wish to compare various shapes of candles to determine which shape is easiest to relight.

Science Concept

You've already read about how a candle burns the wick and the wax. What you may not know is that once the wax burns, it actually turns into a wax vapor that is still flammable. If you bring a lighted match into this stream of flammable wax vapor, the vapor will ignite, and as long as there is still a path to the wick, the flame will travel down to the wick and relight the candle. If you wait too long, you won't be able to do it, but if you time it right you can relight the candle without ever touching the wick.

Materials

- **Various candles of different sizes and shapes**
- **Glass or plastic cylinder to place around the candle. You may also use a lamp chimney if you have one at your house. This experiment can be done without the cylinder, but the results are more impressive if you use it.**

continued on next page

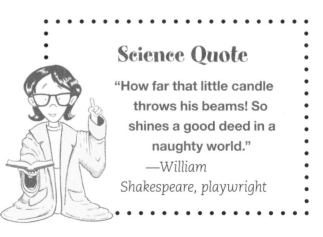

Science Quote

"How far that little candle throws his beams! So shines a good deed in a naughty world."
—William Shakespeare, playwright

Bubble, Bubble, Toil and Trouble

- **2 small wood blocks**
- **Matches**
- **Adult helper**

Procedure

1. Place the two wood blocks on either side of the candle and place the cylinder guard on top of the blocks. This allows air to pass under the guard and feed the flame.
2. Have your adult helper light the candle and let it burn for several minutes.
3. Gently blow out the candle and look for the stream of smoke rising from the wick.
4. Now have your adult helper light another match and place it in the stream of smoke. If you time it right, the flame will travel down to the wick and relight the candle.
5. For the sake of your project, you may wish to change the height of the blocks upon which the guard sits in order to test various heights for relighting the candle. Alternately, you may wish to simply remove the guard and place the lighted match at various heights above the wick.
6. Repeat this experiment as many times as you like, testing various candle sizes and shapes, and various heights above the wick to see which are the most effective for relighting the candle.

Conclusion

Did you know that those magic birthday candles, the ones that relight after they've been blown out, use this same principle? When you blow one out, the wick is still quite hot. It's not hot enough to continue burning the candle, but it is hot enough to light special material that has been placed on the wick, usually magnesium. When you see sparks coming from these candles, you are seeing the magnesium burning. The magnesium, and just afterward, the wick, can be relit with the heat of the wax vapor and the hot wick. This phenomenon, while fascinating to watch, poses a danger to anyone using candles. You see, when you blow out a candle, it's easy to think that the flame is out for good. But as long as the wax vapor still rises off the wick, the candle can be relit if you aren't careful. Be sure all candles are completely extinguished before leaving them, and never leave a burning candle unattended, as it could easily start a fire.

WORDS to KNOW

FLAMMABLE: Capable of catching fire.

Oops!

A scientist invented a powerful liquid that would dissolve anything it touched. Sadly, he couldn't sell his invention. Why not?

Each definition below suggests a word. Write the word on the lines, and then put each letter in its proper place in the grid. Work back and forth between the grid and the answers until you can read the silly answer to the riddle.

A. Small bugs that can infect the hair on your head

$\overline{19}$ $\overline{27}$ $\overline{3}$ $\overline{24}$

B. Flat, square piece of baked clay

$\overline{9}$ $\overline{11}$ $\overline{6}$ $\overline{2}$

C. To rest on top of water

$\overline{10}$ $\overline{26}$ $\overline{4}$ $\overline{14}$ $\overline{28}$

D. The opposite of fat

$\overline{18}$ $\overline{1}$ $\overline{29}$ $\overline{8}$

E. Narrow opening for a coin

$\overline{23}$ $\overline{25}$ $\overline{16}$ $\overline{21}$

F. Tied hand and foot with rope

$\overline{15}$ $\overline{22}$ $\overline{5}$ $\overline{30}$ $\overline{13}$

G. Small boo-boo in a car's fender

$\overline{7}$ $\overline{20}$ $\overline{12}$ $\overline{17}$

1D	2B		3A	4C	5F	6B	7G	8D		9B
		10C	11B	12G	13F		14C			
	15F	16E	17G	18D	19A	20G		21E	22F	
23E	24A	25E	26C		27A	28C		29D	30F	!

Chapter 7

Get Physical!

Physics is a science of practical examples that you see around you every day. In fact, physics is such a part of your day-to-day life, you may not even realize just how much physics you know. For example, when you throw a ball up in the air, do you know that gravity makes it fall back down? Have you ever tried to walk along an icy sidewalk, fallen, and thought about friction? In this chapter, you will explore some unexpected and uncommon examples of how physics is all around you. You will make a glass disappear, have trouble drinking from a straw, and chop out the bottom floor of a building without disturbing the rest of the building.

WORDS to KNOW

FRICTION: The rubbing of one object against another, a force that tends to restrict movement.

INERTIA: The tendency of an object to resist changes in its motion.

Try This: Spinning Eggs

If you like eggs, chances are you have experienced a problem similar to this one: you open the refrigerator and find three eggs on the shelf. The trouble is, you can't tell whether they are raw or hard-boiled. Obviously, you can crack an egg open to see what kind of egg it is, but if it's hard-boiled, and you want it raw, you end up wasting the eggs. On the other hand, if you want it to be hard-boiled, and it turns out to be raw, you will still be wasting an egg, and this time, you'll have a big mess to clean up.

Question: How can you tell a raw egg from a hard-boiled one?

Materials
- 1 raw egg
- 1 hard-boiled egg (You may want to ask an adult to help you prepare the hard-boiled egg.)

Procedure
1. Set both eggs on their sides in front of you.
2. In turn, spin each egg, noticing how fast they spin.

The Science Behind the Magic
You should have noticed that the two eggs spin differently. This is because of iner-

tia. The insides of the raw egg (everything but the eggshell) are not connected to the shell. When you set the egg in motion, the shell tries to spin, but the insides do not. This prevents the whole egg from spinning quickly, and instead, it spins quite slowly. However, a hard-boiled egg is essentially a solid object. So when you spin one, everything inside spins with the shell, and the whole egg spins quickly. This is how you can easily tell what kind of egg you have—raw eggs spin slowly and hard-boiled eggs spin quickly.

Did You Know?

The spinning motion of the insides of a raw egg is not natural. Objects, such as the insides of raw eggs, tend to want to move in a straight line. However, the shell of the egg prevents this, and instead causes the insides to move in a circular motion. This force exerted by the eggshell is called centripetal force.

Follow-Up

Want to see something even more surprising? Try this experiment again, but this time, once each egg is spinning, stop it and immediately let go of it. The hard-boiled egg will stop spinning right away, but the raw egg will actually start spinning again! It does this because while the insides of the egg don't easily start spinning, eventually they do. Once you stop the outer shell, the insides continue spinning for a short time. So if you stop the egg and then let go of the shell quickly, the inertia of the insides of the raw egg will cause it to continue spinning.

Try This: Not So Sip-ple Straw

Imagine it's a hot summer day. You just poured yourself a tall glass of lemonade and can't wait to drink it. You pull out one straw, drink some lemonade, and think, two straws would bring up even more juice faster. So you pull out a second straw, but this time, when you go to drink, you can't get a drop of lemonade up to your mouth. How is this possible?

Question: When is one straw better than two?

Materials
- **Drinking glass**
- **Water**
- **2 identical straws**

Procedure
1. Fill the glass at least half-full with water.
2. Place one straw in the water and drink a mouthful.
3. Add a second straw, but place this straw just outside the glass so that one straw is in the water and one is not.
4. Now try to drink through the two straws.

Science Online

At NASA Space Place site, you can learn about Earth, air, and space with a variety of interactive activities: *http://spaceplace.jpl.nasa.gov/en/kids/cs_earth_moon.shtml.*

The Science Behind the Magic

When you try to suck on a straw, what you are really doing is creating a difference in air pressure between your mouth and the glass of water. Because of this pressure difference, the water flows up the straw from a place of higher pressure (the glass) to lower pressure (your mouth). As soon as you let go of the straw, the pressure equals out and the water falls back into the glass. What happened when you added the second straw was that when you sucked in, you pulled in air from outside the glass and were unable to produce a low-pressure place in your mouth. Instead of pulling water from the glass, you simply pulled air from outside the glass. Try putting both straws into the glass now and see if it works any better.

Get Physical!

Follow-Up

There is a variation on this experiment that you might want to explore. It involves a sharp pin, so you may want to ask an adult to help you.

1. First, refill the glass so it is at least half-full once more.
2. Place a single straw in the glass and drink some water.
3. Have an adult help you poke a small hole in the straw about two inches below the top of the straw.
4. Place the straw back in the water and try drinking again.

You should find that it becomes more difficult to drink water with a hole in the straw. If you were to make the hole even bigger, you would have an even harder time drinking. The reason for this is the same one as before. With a hole in the straw, air is pulled into the straw from the outside, and water is not pulled up from inside the glass.

Science Quote

"There is a single light of science and to brighten it anywhere is to brighten it everywhere."

—*Isaac Asimov, a Russian-born American author and professor of biochemistry*

Which Way?

Question: Can water make an arrow change direction?

Experiment Overview

Light is a remarkable substance. It has no weight; it travels at, well, the speed of light; and it only knows how to move in one direction—straight. But people say light can be bent. How is this possible? In this experiment, you'll be exploring how light can be made to change directions when passing through a container of water. And you will see how this changes the direction of an arrow, or any other object, placed behind the container.

Science Concept

Light travels in straight lines. But when it passes through different materials, it changes speeds, sometimes slowing down when it does so. When a ray of light enters a container of water at an angle, it tends to change direction as it moves through the water, still in a straight line, but in a different straight line from before. This strange behavior of light causes some rays to enter on one side and be "bent" to the extent that they come out the container on the other side. The end result, under the right conditions, is that a right-facing arrow placed behind a container of water can be made to point to the left, when viewed from the other side of the container.

Materials

- **3" x 5" note card**
- **Pen**
- **Clear glass jar or container**
- **Water**

Procedure

1. Draw a horizontal arrow on the note card. Make it large enough that it can be seen from a few feet away.
2. Fill the container with water. You should be able to look through the container and see what is on the other side.
3. Place the arrow you drew on the other side of the container directly behind the container.
4. Look through the container at the arrow and verify that it points in the same direction as it does if you look at it directly.
5. Slowly move the note card away from the container until the arrow changes direction. You may need to enlist the help of an assistant for this step.

Questions for the Scientist

1. When did the arrow point in the same direction as viewed through the water as it did when viewed directly, at a distance or close up?

_____

_____

2. How far from the container was the card when you could first see the reversed arrow?

_____

_____

3. Was there ever a point where the arrow was not visible? In terms of light rays, what does it mean if you cannot see the arrow, even when you know it is located just behind the container of water?

_____

_____

4. Think about glasses that people wear to see. Are there any glasses that cause images to be reversed like this? See if you can find some and experiment with producing reversed images.

_____

_____

Follow-Up

Most people will end up wearing glasses or corrective lenses in their lifetime. Many younger people are nearsighted, which means they can see things up close, but have a hard time seeing things at a distance. As people get older, however, they often need reading glasses. This is because they have become far-sighted, which means they can see things in the distance, but they have trouble reading or seeing things up close. Research the difference in these two types of vision problems and explore the different types of glasses people use to correct them. If you really want to do some research, figure out how glasses prescriptions are written, and what the positive and negative numbers mean. Then try to figure out which type of vision problem positive prescriptions fix, and which negative prescriptions fix.

• • • • • • • • • • • • • • • • •

Awesome Arrows

Are the long lines parallel (even) with each other, or are they crooked?
Do you believe what your eyes are telling you?
Extra Science: Take two straight edges and check the long lines.

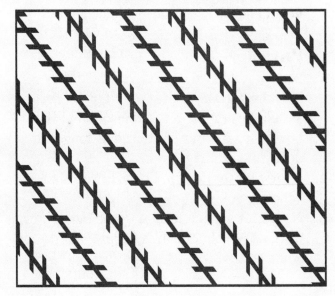

Try This:
Disappearing Glass

We see objects because they are made of different materials. Some materials block light, while others allow light to pass right through. As you just saw, some materials bend light. When you bring two materials together that both allow light to pass and bend light in the same way, sometimes you can make one appear to disappear.

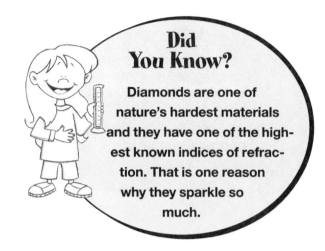

Did You Know?

Diamonds are one of nature's hardest materials and they have one of the highest known indices of refraction. That is one reason why they sparkle so much.

Question: Can you make a glass disappear?

Materials
- **Small Pyrex glass bowl, glass, or cup**
- **Glass bowl that is slightly larger than your Pyrex glass bowl**
- **Vegetable oil**

Procedure
1. Pour at least two cups of vegetable oil into the bottom of the larger bowl. There should be at least 2–3 inches of oil in the bowl. This oil may be reused as long as it does not get dirty.
2. Gently place the Pyrex bowl in the oil. What do you see?
3. Now pour vegetable oil into the Pyrex bowl until it is about one inch deep. What do you see now?

The Science Behind the Magic

What you are seeing is not magic. Instead, it is simply light that passes through certain materials in certain ways. When you look at a Pyrex glass bowl in air, light behaves very differently when it passes through the two materials (Pyrex glass and air). We say that the index of refraction of light and air are different, and this is why they are easy to tell apart. However, vegetable oil and Pyrex glass have very similar indices of refraction. Because of this, light behaves the same way as it passes through oil as it does when it passes through the glass. As a result, we are not able to see a clear boundary between them, and the glass seems to disappear in the oil.

Get Physical!

Follow-Up

Scientists today are trying to invent a way for objects to become "invisible." But that doesn't mean they will simply disappear, like you might see in the movies or on TV. Instead, one idea is to create some sort of shield or article of clothing that has the same index of refraction as its surroundings. If someone figures out how to do this, then anyone wearing this cloaking device could move around and not be detected. Maybe you will be the one to discover how this can be done!

INDEX OF REFRACTION: A measure of how much light is bent in a material.

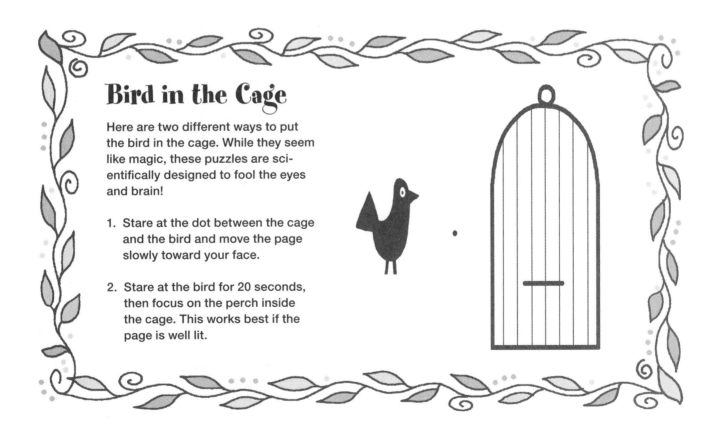

Bird in the Cage

Here are two different ways to put the bird in the cage. While they seem like magic, these puzzles are scientifically designed to fool the eyes and brain!

1. Stare at the dot between the cage and the bird and move the page slowly toward your face.

2. Stare at the bird for 20 seconds, then focus on the perch inside the cage. This works best if the page is well lit.

Removing the Ground Floor

Question: is it possible to knock out a building's ground floor without disturbing the rest of the building?

Experiment Overview

In this experiment, you will be building towers of similar-shaped objects, such as pennies. You will then practice sliding one of those objects at the tower, knocking out the bottom object, and leaving the rest undisturbed. This is another example of inertia at work. The challenge will be hitting the stack just right so that only the bottom object is knocked out. Once you get good at it, you can repeat the task over and over and eventually bring the whole tower down, one floor at a time.

Science Concept

You probably have a lot of pennies at home in a jar. Stack some of them up and examine them. While a stack of pennies may appear to be connected, each penny is actually its own entity. That means that each one moves independent of the others. When the tower is at rest, each penny has its own inertia, which makes it want to stay at rest. According to a law discovered by Sir Isaac Newton, objects at rest tend to stay at rest until an unbalanced force acts on them. When you slide that extra penny into the stack, it produces a force that causes only the bottom penny to change from being at rest to being in motion. The rest of the pennies don't experience this force and therefore stay at rest. This is one reason why it's important that you choose objects that are all the same size.

Materials
- **Several identical items that can easily be stacked, like pennies**
- **A flat, smooth table**

Procedure
1. Form a stack of all your pennies except one. This one remaining penny will be your "shooter."
2. Carefully slide your shooter penny at the stack at a fairly high speed. It must hit the stack hard enough to knock the bottom penny out of the stack. This step may take some practice.
3. Once you have mastered the penny slide, continue knocking out pennies from the bottom of the stack until they are no longer stacked up.

Questions for the Scientist

1. How does this experiment demonstrate Newton's first law that states, "objects at rest tend to stay at rest until acted upon by an unbalanced force?" Describe this in terms of the bottom penny and in terms of the rest of the pennies in the stack.

2. Why did only the bottom penny get knocked out when struck by the shooter penny?

3. Why do you think it is important to use all the same objects in this experiment? For example, why wouldn't you want to mix pennies, nickels, and dimes?

4. Do you think it would be possible to slide a penny just right so that the bottom penny is knocked out but it is replaced by the shooter penny? Try it and see if you can make it work.

5. Do you think you could make a tree shorter in this fashion, by knocking out the bottom part of the tree while the rest of the tree stood untouched? Why or why not?

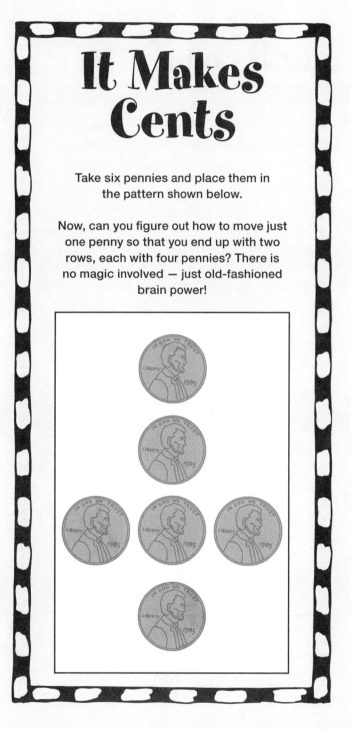

It Makes Cents

Take six pennies and place them in the pattern shown below.

Now, can you figure out how to move just one penny so that you end up with two rows, each with four pennies? There is no magic involved — just old-fashioned brain power!

Science Fair: Finding a Balance

Much of nature is based on balance. When you walk, you maintain balance so you don't fall down. In the wild, animal populations are forced to stay in balance with the supply of food. If the food supply dwindles, the animal population does the same. Your parents spend time each month making sure their check-books are balanced, so there is enough money coming in to equal the money they have to pay for things like bills and food. In physics, find-ing a balance point is often as simple as find-ing the middle of an object. For example, if you were to place a broomstick on the table, you could easily measure from either end to find its middle. That, in all likelihood, would be its bal-ance point, something you could test by hold-ing a finger underneath it at that point to see if it balances. But what if the object you are try-ing to balance is irregular in shape, such as a baseball bat, or a golf club? Could you still find its middle, or center of gravity, simply by mea-suring? This experiment will answer that ques-tion for you and might give you some ideas for how to extend this idea even further.

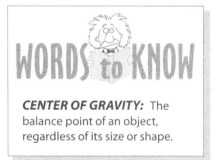

WORDS to KNOW

CENTER OF GRAVITY: The balance point of an object, regardless of its size or shape.

Question: How do you find an object's center of gravity?

Experiment Overview

You will begin with a yardstick (a meter stick is fine, too), and will perform some sim-ple tests to verify that the center of gravity of the stick is indeed in its exact middle. Then you will be adding weight to various locations along the yardstick and will repeat the experi-ment to find the new center of gravity. Once you have mastered the technique with a yard-stick, you will be challenged to try it on irreg-ularly shaped objects you might have lying around your house.

Science Concept

Finding the center of gravity of an object can be very helpful. For example, if you were to swing a baseball bat, you could tell if there was too much weight in the end, and if there was, you could hold the bat farther from the bottom to make up for it. Also, if you had to carry something large and heavy by yourself, you would have to find the center of gravity and make sure it was supported. Otherwise, as soon as you started to carry it, it would twist and fall to the ground.

When working with a plain yardstick, as you move your hands closer to the center, one hand will be holding up more of the yardstick's weight than the other. The second hand will therefore be able to slide toward the center of the stick. However, before long, that second hand will now

Get Physical!

be supporting more of the yardstick's weight, and this will allow the first hand to begin sliding toward the center. Eventually, you will find that both hands will slide to the exact center of the yardstick and it will be balanced at that point. Adding weights or changing to an irregular shape will not change this process.

Materials
- **Yardstick**
- **Molding clay**
- **Various irregularly shaped objects, preferably long and fairly thin (A baseball bat would be a good example.)**

Procedure
1. Hold the yardstick in front of you, resting on your two index fingers. Your index fingers should be placed near the ends of the yardstick.
2. With your eyes closed, slowly move your two index fingers toward the center of the yardstick. They will take turns sliding, one stopping while the other slides, and then the first beginning to slide. They should meet in the center of the yardstick.
3. Try this experiment again, placing your fingers at different locations to begin with. Convince yourself that they will always meet in the exact middle of the yardstick.
4. Now form a palm-sized ball of clay and place it somewhere on the yardstick other than the middle.

5. Repeat step 2 until your fingers meet. This is the new center of gravity of the yardstick. You can confirm this by the fact that the stick balances when your fingers are placed there.
6. Repeat steps 4 and 5 with various amounts of clay, placing them at various locations on the yardstick. Each time, your fingers should end up at the center of gravity of your yardstick.

Questions for the Scientist
1. After completing this experiment, give a definition in your own words for the phrase "center of gravity."

   _____

   _____

2. After placing a ball of clay on the yardstick, try to predict the center of gravity that it will produce. How close was your prediction?

   _____

   _____

3. Why do you suppose your fingers do not slide at the same time, but instead take turns sliding toward the center of the stick?

   _____

   _____

4. In what sorts of situations, other than those listed here, would it be helpful to know an object's center of gravity?

_____

_____

5. In addition to weight, what other factors might affect the amount of friction your fingers experience?

_____

_____

6. Can you think of an object for which this process would not work?

_____

_____

Conclusion

Knowing the center of gravity of anything that is manufactured, from a baseball bat to a golf club, makes it more reliable, and safer and easier to use. Engineers work very hard to make sure that products they design and build are balanced, easy to operate, and safe for those who buy them. For example, if a car's center of gravity is located too high above the road, it could easily tip over when turning a corner. See if you can look for other ways to find the center of gravity of objects you encounter every day. You may be surprised at how easy it is to do once you know what you are looking for.

Did You Know?

All cars can roll over, but the taller a car is the more likely it is to be involved in a roll-over accident. Forty percent of roll-over accidents in which someone dies involve excessive speeding.

Chapter 8
Wind and Weather

Each night on the news, a meteorologist presents the day's weather and gives predictions for the next day. In that report, viewers often hear about high and low temperatures, winds, and any rain or snow that may have fallen. You may hear people talk about temperatures, wind speeds, and rain, but do they really know what weather is all about? This isn't a book about weather, but in this chapter, you will explore air and how it behaves in all kinds of situations. You will create an air cannon, seal a leaking balloon, make cereal float, and create an imploding time bomb.

Try This: Air Cannon

Some people hear the word *cannon* and automatically think about something violent, used in times of war or for celebrating a score at an athletic event. But this cannon is perfectly safe and can actually help you impress your friends while performing some amazing feats.

Question: How can you blow out a candle from across the room?

Science Online

The original air cannon was called the Air Blaster, made by the Wham-O toy company. It was introduced in 1965, and you can learn more about Wham-O at their Web site. Follow the "About Us" link to read about the company's long history of innovative toys: *www.wham-o.com*.

Materials
- Clean 8-ounce yogurt container
- Adult helper
- Scissors or knife
- Medium balloon
- Rubber band
- Lit candle

Procedure
1. Ask your adult helper to cut a small hole in the bottom of the yogurt container. The hole should be approximately one-half inch in diameter.
2. Cut the mouth off the balloon and stretch it across the top opening of the yogurt container. Secure the balloon to the mouth of the container with the rubber band.
3. Tap on the balloon to produce a small burst of air out the hole in the bottom of the container.
4. Bring your air cannon near the candle and tap on the balloon until you can make the candle go out.

The Science Behind the Magic

When you tap on the balloon, you compress all the air in the container. As the volume of the air decreases, the pressure inside the container increases. All that air has to go somewhere, so it gets pushed out the hole in the bottom. As the air passes through the small hole, it picks up speed. The air comes out of the hole as a vortex, and it tends to keep its form and can travel surprising distances across a room.

Follow-Up

See how far you can move from the candle and still blow it out using your air cannon. Some cannons have been known to work from across an entire room. You can also set up paper cups on a table as targets and practice knocking them over. Be careful when using your air cannon around people or pets, however. An unexpected blast of air is not always a welcome surprise. Several versions of this air cannon are possible, including one you can purchase at many toy stores. But you can experiment with building larger versions yourself. You can try using a tin can, such as one that would hold soup, vegetables, or dog food. Or you could use a larger can, such as one that would hold canned tomatoes. If you really want to upgrade your air cannon, try making one out of a plastic bucket or garbage can. You will need to experiment with various materials in place of the balloon, but the larger you make your cannon, the farther its bursts of air will travel.

Bowling with Air

This young scientist used an air cannon to knock over three towers of paper cups. With which tower did she get the highest score? Count only the paper cups that have fallen on the table.

Extra Fun: If the scientist tries again, and knocks over two more cups in each tower, what is the highest score she can get?

Try This: Floating Cereal

Cereal is a common breakfast food, one that is quick and easy, and also can be very nutritious. But chances are you didn't know it also can serve as a magical science experiment. Because of a relationship discovered by Daniel Bernoulli, air has the ability not only to lift up a piece of your favorite cereal, but keep it floating off the table as long as you can provide the air.

Question: Does cereal float?

Materials
- **Spherical pieces of your favorite cereal**
- **Drinking straw that bends near the top**

Procedure
1. Bend the upper part of the straw so it makes an L-shape.
2. Place your mouth at the long end of the straw with the bent end pointing up into the air.
3. While you blow through the straw, place one piece of cereal just above the far end, where the air is exiting the straw.
4. Try to balance the piece of cereal above your straw while you blow through it. With practice you should be able to control the height at which the cereal floats above the straw.

The Science Behind the Magic
Daniel Bernoulli discovered that in a stream of moving air, the pressure is lower

WORDS to KNOW

BERNOULLI PRINCIPLE:
When a substance, including air, speeds up, the pressure decreases.

than in the air outside the stream that is not moving. While the piece of cereal is in the stream of air, it stays in a position of lower air pressure. As it drifts toward the edge of the moving air stream, it hits the air with higher pressure and is pushed back into the stream. As long as the air stream remains, the cereal will stay "stuck" in the stream and will float.

Follow-Up
You can explore this idea on a larger scale by setting a hair dryer on a table so that it points upward. Turn it on and place a Ping-Pong ball in the air stream above the hair dryer. It should float. The Bernoulli Principle doesn't just make small objects fly, however. It is one factor that helps airplanes fly. If you research the shape of an airplane's wings, you'll see that they are designed so that air travels faster over the top of the wings than below. This creates an area of lower pressure above the wing, which helps the airplane stay in the air. Can you find other places this principle shows up? It might surprise you to see just how common it is.

The Uninflating Balloon

Experiment Overview

This experiment explores the fact that air takes up space. You may not be able to see it, but it's there and this experiment will demonstrate that. The goal will be to blow up a balloon inside a plastic bottle. But in the first version of this experiment, you will first attempt to inflate the balloon without placing anything else inside the bottle. You will then add a straw to see if it has any effect on your ability to blow up the balloon. In the second version, the bottle will first be untouched and then will have a small hole placed in it. Your task will be to determine whether that hole has any effect on your ability to inflate the balloon.

Science Concept

Air takes up space. You actually demonstrate this every time you take a breath. As you breathe in, your lungs expand to hold the air. When you breathe out that air, your chest and lungs deflate a little bit. In this case, you are dealing with air that already resides inside the bottle. When you try to put air into the balloon, it has to displace the air already in the bottle. With no exit path available—this happens in the first test when nothing is added to the bottle, and in the second when no hole is present in the bottle—the existing air stays right where it is and it becomes impossible for the balloon to inflate. However, by adding the straw, the air now has a path to

travel and it can escape. This makes room for the new air you are breathing into the balloon and it easily inflates. With a hole in the bottom of the bottle, the air inside the bottle just escapes out the hole and this is what allows the balloon to inflate.

Materials

- **2 (20-ounce or 1-liter) plastic bottles**
- **Drinking straw**
- **Thumbtack**
- **Medium balloon**

Procedures

PART I

1. Place the balloon inside the bottle with its mouth sticking out the top of the bottle.
2. Blow into the mouth of the balloon and try to inflate it. You should find it very difficult to do.
3. Now place the straw next to the balloon inside the bottle. Be sure that the end of the straw sticks out of the mouth of the bottle.

4. Try inflating the balloon again. You should find it much easier to do so.

PART II
1. As before, place the balloon inside the bottle with its mouth sticking out the top of the bottle.
2. Blow into the mouth of the balloon and try to inflate it. You should find it very difficult to do.
3. Using the thumbtack, poke a small hole, about the size of a nail hole, in the bottom of the bottle.
4. Now when you try to inflate the balloon by blowing into its mouth, it should inflate easily.

Questions for the Scientist

1. Why did the balloon not inflate initially in either of the tests?

_____
_____
_____

2. Where did the air you blew into the balloons go in both tests?

_____
_____
_____

3. The straw and the hole you made in the bottle allowed air to escape from the bottle. Where did this air come from?

_____
_____
_____

4. If you are blowing air into the balloon and air is escaping through the straw or hole, how does the balloon inflate?

_____
_____
_____

I Can't See You

Start at the letter marked with a dot. Collect every other letter around the circle, clockwise, until you have them all. You will need to go around twice! Read the letters in order to find out what this scientist has discovered.

We didn't tell you which way to go around the circle — you will have to discover that by yourself!

When are your eyes not your eyes?

H E E M W W I

H

A

T

N

T

T

D

N

E

S

M

E

E H K W. A R

Try This: Balloon Cents

Don't you hate it when you have a balloon all blown up and it unexpectedly springs a leak? All your work is wasted, and try as you might, it's nearly impossible to reinflate a balloon once it's been deflated. But this time you will actually be able to repair a hole in a balloon, hopefully before all the air leaks out. Granted, the fix won't last forever, but it will do the trick for a while at least.

Question: Can you repair a leak in a balloon?

Materials
- **Medium latex balloon**
- **Penny**
- **Vegetable oil**
- **Small needle or pin**

Procedure
1. Place the penny inside the balloon before inflating it.
2. Inflate the balloon so that it is more than halfway, but not all the way, inflated. Tie off the end.
3. Practice swinging the balloon around so that the penny inside spins around the inside of the balloon. You can best do this by holding the balloon near the knot and letting it hang down.
4. Dip the needle in oil and carefully insert it into the end of the balloon opposite the knot. Remove the needle, leaving a small hole.
5. While holding the balloon as before, allow the penny to align itself over the hole in the end of the balloon.
6. Slowly turn the balloon right side up and the penny should stay in place, effectively sealing the hole.

The Science Behind the Magic

Try as you might to seal a hole in a balloon from the outside, it will most likely fail. Some people try to use a piece of tape, or glue, or other adhesive. But the air inside typically pushes against the seal and the hole stays unpatched. But the penny seals the hole from within because of the difference in air pressure inside the balloon compared to outside the balloon. When you blew up the balloon, you filled it with air that is compressed inside. This produces more air pressure inside than outside. As a result, when the penny is allowed to cover the hole, the higher air pressure inside the balloon pushes outward on the penny, keeping it in place over the hole and preventing any more air from leaking out.

Follow-Up

There are a number of variations of this experiment that you can try. For example, you can try other coins to see which are most effective at sealing holes. You can also try dipping the coins in different liquids, such as oil or water, to see if the addition of those liquids forms a tighter seal than the coin alone. Another option is to try poking the hole in different places on the balloon. Is there a reason why you were instructed to make the hole at the end opposite the knot? Finally, you can time the experiments to see just how long the penny seal holds. If you work at it, you might be able to perfect the sealing technique and it could lead to a new way to fix leaking tires!

Did You Know?

The latex in most rubber balloons comes from the sap of a special kind of tree called a rubber tree, which grows in Malaysia.

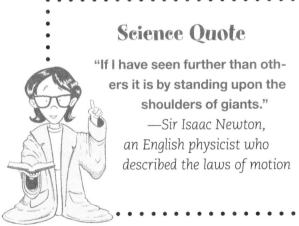

Science Quote

"If I have seen further than others it is by standing upon the shoulders of giants."
—Sir Isaac Newton, an English physicist who described the laws of motion

Peeling a Banana

Question: How do you peel a banana without using your hands?

Experiment Overview

Peeling a banana isn't the most difficult task ever. But wouldn't it be amazing to be able to watch a banana peel itself? You can, with this activity. You will have to open the top of the banana, just enough to reveal part of the fruit inside. Then you will rely on a difference in air pressure to do the rest of the work for you.

Science Concept

You have already seen a few situations where higher air pressure causes something to be pushed toward lower air pressure. In this experiment, the burning paper uses up some of the available air in the bottle. With less air inside the bottle, the outside air pressure will push the banana down into the bottle. By opening the peel slightly, you allow the banana to be pushed down into the bottle and peel itself.

SAFETY NOTE: When this experiment is complete, the banana will be covered in smoke and perhaps burnt paper. Please do not eat any food item used in a science experiment.

Materials

- **Glass bottle with a mouth approximately as large as a banana**
- **1 ripe banana that, when peeled, is about the same size as the mouth of the bottle**
- **Small piece of paper**
- **Matches or a lighter**
- **Adult helper**

Procedure

1. Peel back the tip of the banana, exposing the fruit inside.
2. Ask your adult helper to carefully light the paper and slide it inside the bottle. Alternately, your helper may be able to place the paper inside the bottle and use the long tip of a lighter to start the paper burning.
3. Place the banana, exposed side down, into the mouth of the bottle. Be sure there are no air holes around the banana.
4. As the paper burns itself out, watch as the banana begins to peel itself.

Questions for the Scientist

1. It's possible that the flame went out before the paper was completely burned. Why do you think this happened?

   _____

   _____

   _____

   _____

2. Describe what happened to the banana after the flame went out.

   _____

   _____

   _____

   _____

3. Why do you think the difference in air pressure causes the banana to be pulled down into the bottle?

   _____

   _____

   _____

   _____

4. Why is it important that there are no air holes at the mouth of the bottle? What might happen in this experiment if there were (air holes)?

   _____

   _____

   _____

   _____

Science Fair: Canned Water

Everyone knows that to store water in a jar, you simply open the lid and pour it in. But if you turn the jar upside down, you'll have a big mess on your hands. No one wants a puddle of water on the floor, so instead, you can try this experiment. By reducing the air pressure inside the jar, you can pull water up into the jar and keep it there. What's more, you can test different jars and different types of candles to see which combination draws the most water up into the jar.

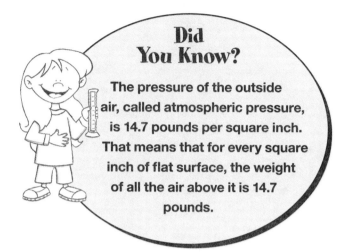

Did You Know?

The pressure of the outside air, called atmospheric pressure, is 14.7 pounds per square inch. That means that for every square inch of flat surface, the weight of all the air above it is 14.7 pounds.

Question: How can a candle fill a jar with water?

Experiment Overview

In this experiment, you will place a candle in a pan of water. You will then light the candle and cover it with a glass jar. When the flame goes out, the water will magically be sucked up into the jar. Until you remove the jar from the pan, the water will stay there. You task is to test various candle shapes, sizes, and heights, to see which allows the greatest amount of water to be sucked up into the jar. You will also be able to test different types of jars (glass only) to see whether jar shape has any effect on the amount of water that can be pulled up. Be sure when doing this experiment that you only change one variable at a time. If you change more than one part of your experi-

ment, you won't know which one caused the effect you observe.

Science Concept

We know that gravity makes objects fall to the ground. In general, water obeys this law. However, when the pressure is strong enough, water can actually overcome the effects of gravity and move upward into the jar. This only happens when the air inside the jar is removed or reduced to the point that outside air pressure can push the water up into the jar. Atmospheric pressure is constantly pushing down on the water in the pan. If you were to place the jar over an unlit candle, the pressure on the water inside the jar would be the same as the pressure on the water outside the jar. Only when the candle burns up and consumes some of the oxygen inside the jar does the air pressure inside drop. This lower air pressure cannot overcome the outside air pressure and the water is forced up into the jar.

Materials

- **Glass or metal pie plate**
- **Several glass bottles of different heights and diameters**
- **Several candles of various sizes, shapes, and heights**
- **Water**
- **Marking pen**

Procedure

1. Fill the pie plate with water.
2. Place the candle in the middle of the plate, taking care that the top of the candle sits above the surface of the water.
3. Place the jar, mouth down, over the candle to verify that the water level inside the jar is the same as the water level outside the jar.
4. Remove the jar and light the candle.
5. Replace the jar over the candle. Watch as the candle goes out and the water is sucked up into the jar.
6. When the water level inside the jar stops rising, use your pen to mark the water height.
7. Carefully remove the jar from the water. The extra water in the jar will pour back into the pie plate.
8. Repeat steps 2–6, either with a different candle or a different jar. Each time you produce a new mark on the jar, record the diameter and height of the jar and candle.
9. When you have completed all your tests, analyze your data to determine which combination of jar and candle produced the greatest effect on the water.

Questions for the Scientist

1. What type of jar was the most effective for drawing water up in this experiment?

2. How might the jar diameter mislead you to think that one jar pulled up less water than another, when in fact it may have pulled more?

3. What type of candle was most effective for drawing water up in this experiment?

_____

4. What effect might the water temperature have on your results in this experiment? Would warm water react differently than cold water?

_____

Conclusion

You can build a home version of a barometer using a setup similar to this one. By placing a bottle inside a container of water, you can measure the changes in the water height each day as the atmospheric pressure changes. The higher the atmospheric pressure, the higher the water will rise inside the bottle. This concept is similar to the way atmospheric pressure is reported by television news. You may hear something like this: the pressure is 29.9 inches and rising. This is actually a measure of how high mercury would rise in a formal barometer. Good weather is typically associated with high pressure, while lower pressure often brings bad weather. In your experiment, the lower pressure inside the jar made the outside air pressure seem "high," which caused the water to rise into the jar.

Funny Forecast

How do you use a rope to tell the weather?

Meteorologists use a lot of high-tech scientific equipment to predict the weather. But you can use something much more simple — a piece of rope! To find out how this "magic" weather predictor works, figure out where the puzzle pieces go, and write the letters into the empty grid.

Biology is sometimes described as the study of life and living things. Perhaps the most magical thing in all of science is the way living creatures are born and live their lives. You may have experienced the birth of a baby brother or sister, or witnessed the birth of a litter of puppies. More likely, you may have planted a seed and waited for it to grow, celebrating the day when the tiny leaves first appeared above the dirt. In this chapter you will grow a pocket garden, make dyes from different plants, and watch microbes grow in rotting food.

WORDS to KNOW

MICROBE: A tiny life form.

EXTRACT: To separate or draw out from something.

Try This:
Planting a Dye Job

Have you ever wondered where they get the colors for the clothes you wear? What about the paint on the walls of your house? Those colors have to come from somewhere, and something. In many cases, that something is a plant. In this activity, you will get to dye some eggs using common plants.

Question: Do plants contain colors?

Materials
- **Several eggs**
- **Pan of water**
- **Stove**
- **Vinegar**
- **Various plants, such as:**
    - -Mint leaves
    - -Red cabbage
    - -Thyme
    - -Spinach leaves
    - -Golden delicious apple peels
    - -Onion skins
- **Adult helper**

SAFETY NOTE: Don't eat any of the eggs or drink any of the water you produce in this experiment. It may look safe, but you should never eat or drink any part of a science experiment, as you cannot be sure it is safe.

It's Alive!

Procedure

1. With an adult's help, heat the pan of water until it simmers.
2. Add one teaspoon of vinegar.
3. Select one of the plants from the list above and place it in the pot. The more you use, the darker the color will be on the egg.
4. Place the egg in the pan and allow it to simmer for at least 20 minutes.
5. Remove the egg and observe the coloring on its shell.
6. Repeat steps 1–5 for additional plants of your choosing.

The Science Behind the Magic

When you boil certain plants in water, the color comes out of them and goes into the water. The vinegar in the pan makes it easier for the color to bond to the shell of the egg. If you have ever colored eggs for Easter, you may remember using vinegar with the coloring kit. It was for the same reason. This process of extracting dyes from plants and using it to color objects has been around for a very long time. By combining different plants, you may be able to produce new colors.

Follow-Up

The list of plants in this activity is only a beginning. Try this experiment with plants or leaves of your own choosing and see which colors you can produce. You can also replace the egg with a piece of white cotton, such as an old T-shirt, and use the dyes to color your clothing!

Science Quote

"The most exciting phrase to hear in science, the one that heralds new discoveries, is not 'Eureka!' (I found it) but 'That's funny...'"
—*Isaac Asimov*

Did You Know?

Hot tea is made using this same idea. Not only is the color extracted of the tea leaves, but the flavor is also.

Try This: Pocket Garden

Everyone knows that a garden requires a large amount of dirt and plenty of room for the plants to grow, right? Well, not really. True, most people who plant gardens do use a good amount of dirt and require quite a bit of space. But you can grow a garden right in your pocket, and you can check on its progress anytime you like.

Question: Can you grow a garden in your pocket?

Materials
- 1 sealable plastic sandwich bag
- Paper towel
- Water
- 1 bean seed
- At least 1 pocket

Procedure
1. Moisten the paper towel with water and fold it so it fits inside the sandwich bag.
2. Place the bean seed in the sandwich bag and seal the bag. Remove enough of the air so that the bag will fit inside your pants or coat pocket.
3. Place the sandwich bag in your pocket and keep it there for the next week. When you change your clothes, simply transfer the bag to a new pocket.
4. Once or twice a day for the next week, take the bag out and look for signs that the seed is germinating.

The Science Behind the Magic

When you plant a seed in the ground, it doesn't get very much light—it's underground. What it needs is water and time to grow. By placing the seed inside a bag with the moist paper towel, it gets the moisture it needs. By keeping the bag inside a pocket, it gets the dark that it needs. Over the course of a week, you should begin to see signs of the seed sprouting and starting to grow into a plant. The environment inside the bag in your pocket is pretty similar to the environment under the ground, so you can see the whole process from start to finish. Once the seed has germinated, you can try transferring it to a pot or garden with soil to watch it continue its growth.

Follow-Up

The most obvious way to extend this experiment is to test out several kinds of seeds to see which grows best in this "pocket environment." But you can also try placing the bag in different places, including a spot that gets a lot of sunlight, or one that gets no light at all, and one that is very warm, or one that is very cold. By changing the environment for your growing seed, you may be able to determine which combination is the most effective for growing that seed. Can every seed grow without being planted in dirt? Do all seed types require the same kind of environment to grow?

Big Beans

Sometimes, folks really DO use magic to help their garden grow!

See if you can find the correct path from Jack, down the beanstalk, to the correct magic bean.

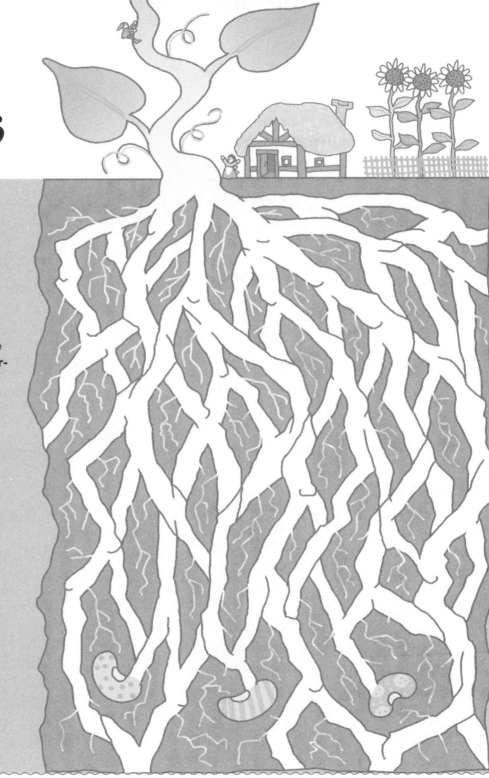

Spicy Seeds

Question: What sorts of spices do seeds prefer?

Experiment Overview

You probably already know that when planting seeds, the right combination of soil, water, and environment helps the seeds grow their very best. What you may not know is that some seeds like it hot and spicy, while others prefer things to be a little milder. In this experiment, you will be growing seeds in soil that has had different spices added to it. You'll be able to compare the effects each spice has on the growth rate of the seeds, and you just might discover a new, safe form of fertilizer that you can use in your own garden.

Science Concept

Plants need more than just dirt and water to grow. That's like saying that people need food and drink to be healthy. It's more than that. People need to have good food and good drink to be healthy. They need the nutrients in what they eat, and plants need the nutrients in the dirt in order to grow. If seeds are planted in dirt that doesn't have the proper nutrients, such as nitrogen, phosphorous, and potassium, they won't grow well. Many people use fertilizer on their plants. Fertilizer provides those nutrients, along with many others, in a form that plants can use. This experiment will test to see if certain spices, commonly available in kitchens, can provide the added benefit that fertilizer does.

Materials

- **Several sealable plastic sandwich bags**
- **Paper towel**
- **Water**
- **Cucumber or other small seeds**
- **Various spices**
- **Dirt**

Procedure

1. Wet several sheets of paper towel and fold them so that each fits inside its own sandwich bag.
2. Add ½ cup of dirt to each sandwich bag.
3. For each bag, select one spice and add one teaspoon of the spice to the dirt inside. Shake the bag to mix up the spice and the dirt.
4. Insert two seeds into each sandwich bag and seal the bag.

5. Over the course of one to two weeks, track the growth of the seeds in each bag, taking care to note the differences in size of the seeds each time you make an observation.

6. If you wish to test other seeds, simply repeat steps 1–5 for each type of seed.

Questions for the Scientist

1. Did you find that one spice had a greater effect on the growth of the seed than the others?

_____

_____

_____

2. Did any spices cause the seed not to grow?

_____

_____

_____

3. What might it mean in terms of the ingredients of a spice if it caused the seed not to grow?

_____

_____

_____

4. Do you think your spices caused the seeds to grow on their own, or do you think that the spices pulled the nutrients the seeds needed out of the dirt?

_____

_____

_____

5. Would you recommend any of your spices as a safe fertilizer?

_____

_____

6. What do you think would happen to the seeds if you were to combine spices in the same growing container?

_____

_____

_____

Follow-Up

To extend this experiment, think about other ways you could plant the seeds to see how they will grow. You might try using small planters, paper cups, saucers with only water, etc. This is very similar to the way many fertilizers are discovered and developed. By testing to see which ones cause the most growth, and which ones have no effect or even bad effects on the seeds, the company that makes them can decide which combinations work best. Another test you could run would be to use just one spice, but vary the amount you add to each seed. Finally, you might also try growing different kinds of seeds to determine whether certain spices work better with certain seeds.

Try This: Rotting Food

Sometimes food gets put into the refrigerator...and forgotten. Unlucky is the person who opens the container of this forgotten food, only to discover that it has turned into something smelly and unappetizing. But to a scientist, this change from dinner to disgusting offers a glimpse into a world that many people don't even know about. Air and food are filled with tiny creatures called microbes. In this experiment, you will let various types of food rot so you can watch the microbes that feed on the food grow.

WORDS to KNOW

ORGANISM: A living thing that is able to act independently.

Question: What do microbes like to eat?

Materials
- **Several sealable plastic sandwich bags**
- **1 slice of cheese**
- **1 piece of sandwich bread**
- **1 piece of fruit, such as an apple, banana, or orange**
- **1 slice of lunch meat**
- **Tap water**

Procedure

1. Set each of the test food items on a plate and let them sit at room temperature for 30–45 minutes.
2. Place each food item in its own plastic sandwich bag.
3. Add two tablespoons of tap water to each bag and seal the bag. Be sure to capture some air inside each bag.
4. Place the sandwich bags in a warm location where they will not be disturbed for up to one week.
5. Check the bags each day for signs of microbe growth. You may want to use a magnifying glass to see these tiny organisms up close.

The Science Behind the Magic

Microbes are everywhere. They live in the air and in the food we eat. Most are harmless, but in large quantities, they turn good food into rotten food. By selecting a variety of foods to test, you should have seen that some foods attract microbes more than others, and perhaps you even see different types of microbes growing in each bag. Microbes love to eat food, and they also like warm, moist places. When you place food in the refrigerator, the colder temperature and the drier air tends to prevent microbes from growing quickly. But even food left in the refrigerator can experience microbe growth over time, as anyone who has discovered a container of forgotten food can tell you.

It's Alive!

Follow-Up

Now that you have an idea of what microbes look like when they grow, and what kinds of food they like, can you think of other foods to test? Look around your kitchen—and always ask your parents' permission before testing new foods—and see what you can find to test. You can also try exposing foods to different temperatures or varying the amount of water you place inside the bag as you extend this idea a little further. Be careful, though. Rotting food doesn't usually smell very nice, and it can make a big mess if it spills out. So be sure to throw away the bags once you have finished with them.

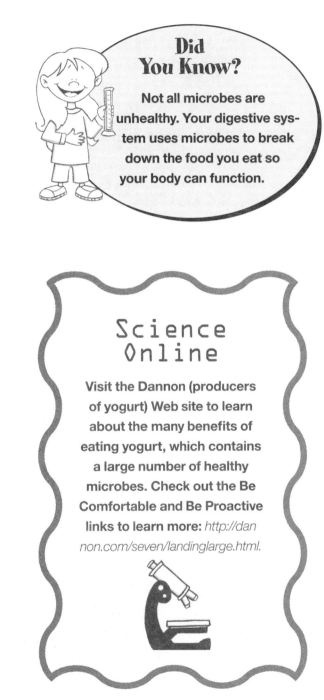

Did You Know?

Not all microbes are unhealthy. Your digestive system uses microbes to break down the food you eat so your body can function.

Science Online

Visit the Dannon (producers of yogurt) Web site to learn about the many benefits of eating yogurt, which contains a large number of healthy microbes. Check out the Be Comfortable and Be Proactive links to learn more: *http://dannon.com/seven/landinglarge.html.*

No Crying over Spoiled Milk

KIDS' LAB LESSONS

Question: What does milk look like when it spoils?

Experiment Overview

In this experiment, you will be comparing several types of milk to see how they change as they spoil over time. White milk comes in several varieties, including skim, 2%, and whole. You can also buy chocolate milk and make milk from a dry mix. You will prepare several jars, each with its own kind of milk, and then you will observe them each day for at least one week to see how they change. It will be important that you label the jars properly so that you can easily observe and record the changes you see.

Science Concept

Milk is a complex combination of water, nutrients such as calcium, and...bacteria. The bacteria that live in milk are not usually harmful at all. In fact, you can typically find these bacteria living in cheese, yogurt, and other dairy products. However, it's important that these bacteria be kept at a certain level. If there are too many of them, the milk can spoil and then it becomes foul-tasting and possibly harmful. Refrigeration helps keep bacteria

populations from growing. Also, boiling milk kills many of the bacteria it contains, which helps keep the bacteria population down. But if you simply leave milk out at room temperature, the bacteria will multiply rapidly and soon the milk will spoil.

Materials

- **Several small sealable containers, such as baby food jars, with lids**
- **½ cup of the following types of milk (or others if you have access to them):**
    - -Skim milk
    - -2% milk
    - -Whole milk
    - -Chocolate (or other flavor) milk
    - -Buttermilk
    - -Milk made from a dry mix
    - -White milk that has been boiled for at least 5 minutes
- **Small strips of paper (to be used as labels)**
- **Tape**
- **Marking pen**
- **Adult helper**

Procedure

1. Prepare each of the jars with its own type of milk.
2. Use refrigerated milk in all cases except for the one made from a mix and the one you boil.
3. Ask your adult helper to boil the white milk you chose for at least five minutes.
4. Write a label on a strip of paper for each type of milk you are testing and attach it to the proper jar with tape.
5. Each day for one week, observe each jar. Make a note of any changes you see in the milk, and any signs that the milk is beginning to spoil.
6. *Optional:* If you wish, each time you make an observation, you may open the jars briefly to see if the milk inside has started to smell. Be careful, though. This step may produce some very strong and unpleasant odors, and is best done outdoors. Be sure to seal the jars firmly after this step.

Questions for the Scientist

1. What sort of changes did you notice in the milk?

   _____

   _____

2. Which type of milk changed the most?

   _____

   _____

3. Did any of the types of milk start to form into solid pieces? Were you able to identify anything these types of milk had in common?

   _____

   _____

4. Which of the types of milk smelled the strongest as they began to spoil?

   _____

   _____

5. Did the boiled milk experience the same kinds of changes that its refrigerated counterpart experienced?

   _____

   _____

6. How long do you think milk should be allowed to sit out on the counter before being placed back into the refrigerator?

   _____

   _____

7. Why do you think people store food in the refrigerator?

   _____

   _____

   _____

Magic Math

Look at the fraction below each blank. Pick the shape that shows that fraction, using these rules: the white part of each shape is empty; the shaded part of each shape is full.

Write the letter of that shape on the line. When you are done, you will have the answer to the riddle!

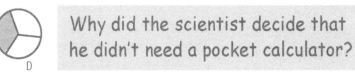

Why did the scientist decide that he didn't need a pocket calculator?

$\overline{}$ $\overline{}$ $\overline{}$ $\overline{}$ $\overline{}$ $\overline{}$ $\overline{}$ $\overline{}$ $\overline{}$ $\overline{}$ $\overline{}$ $\overline{}$ $\overline{}$ $\overline{}$ $\overline{}$ $\overline{}$
2/3 3/4   1/4 4/5 3/6 3/4 1/4 1/3 3/8   2/5 2/4 3/4 1/5   2/3 2/2 1/5

$\overline{}$ $\overline{}$ $\overline{}$ $\overline{}$ $\overline{}$ $\overline{}$ $\overline{}$ $\overline{}$ $\overline{}$ $\overline{}$ $\overline{}$ $\overline{}$ $\overline{}$ $\overline{}$ $\overline{}$ $\overline{}$
1/2 1/4 2/4 3/8   2/6 2/2 5/6 2/5 3/4 4/7 3/5   2/3 3/4   2/3 1/4 1/3

Science Fair: How Does Your Garden Grow?

Each year, families around the world spend lots of money buying just the right plants, just the right soil, and just the right fertilizer that they hope will make those plants grow in that soil. Gardening is a multibillion-dollar-a-year business, so you would think they would have it all figured out by now. But in this experiment, you will have an opportunity to test out your own form of plant care—one that might revolutionize the industry.

Question: What do seeds like to drink?

Experiment Overview

In this experiment you will be growing seeds. That by itself isn't all that magical. But what makes this experiment unique is that you will be "watering" your seeds with more than just water. In fact, it is totally up to you to decide which liquids you will use to keep your seeds moist. You will probably want to include regular water for comparison, but you may find that your own special recipe, or something as common as what you have sitting in your refrigerator, on your dinner table, or in the glass in your hand, actually makes seeds grow better than water.

Did You Know?

In the United States, most beans can be planted and harvested within 90 to 120 days. Michigan, North Dakota, Nebraska, and California are the leading bean-producing states.

Science Concept

Seeds need a lot of things to go right for them in order to grow. They need the right kind of soil, the right amount of light (or darkness), the right temperature, and of course, water. Water helps the seed gather nutrients from the soil, and helps those nutrients work through the growing seed. Fertilizers either deliver additional nutrients that the soil is not able to provide, or they help the seeds gather in the soil's nutrients in a more efficient manner. Some additives, such as chemicals or acids, get in the way of the nutrients the seed needs, and prevent the seed from growing. Others actually help this process along. Which of your liquid additives will do the most for your seeds?

Materials
- **10–20 bean seeds**
- **Several Styrofoam coffee cups**

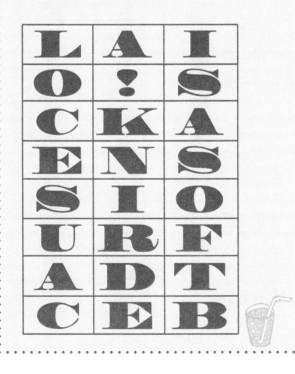

Landing Gear

To find the silly answer to this riddle, start in one corner of the grid. Read the letters one after the other as you spiral around the grid and into the center. The trick is to figure out in which corner to start, and in which direction to read!

A scientist jumped from a high place into a glass of cola that was sitting on the floor. He didn't get hurt — why not?

L	A	I
O	?	S
C	K	A
E	N	S
S	I	O
U	R	F
A	D	T
C	E	B

- Potting soil
- Measuring spoons
- Marking pen
- Ruler
- A variety of liquids, possibly including the following:

-Tap water	-Milk
-Hot water	-Fruit juice
-Iced tea	-Soda
-Hot tea	-Vinegar
-Coffee	-Cooking oil

Procedure

1. Fill each cup about ½ full with potting soil.
2. Place 2–3 seeds in each cup.
3. Cover seeds with another ½–1 inch of potting soil.
4. Select a liquid and pour 1–3 tablespoons of that liquid into the cup.
5. Write the name of the liquid on the side of the cup.
6. Repeat steps 4 and 5 until all liquids have been assigned.
7. Place the cups in a safe, warm place where you can observe the seeds as they grow.
8. Once a day for the next two weeks (14 days), add another three tablespoons of each liquid to the proper cup.
9. Each time you add liquid, look for growth of the seeds in the cup. After two weeks, there should be measurable growth from many of the seeds that you can record with the ruler. Save these measurements in a data table for reference.

It's Alive!

Questions for the Scientist

1. Which of your liquids produced the greatest growth in your seeds?

   _____

2. Did any of your liquids cause the seeds not to grow at all?

   _____

3. How did water do in comparison to the other liquids? Can you suggest a better alternative to tap water for growing seeds?

   _____

4. What ingredients did your test liquids have that might have caused the seeds to grow more slowly or not at all?

   _____

5. Can you think of any combinations of the liquids you tested that might work even better?

   _____

Conclusion

Acids, such as those found in vinegar or carbonated soda, tend to slow down the growth of seeds. Other liquids contain chemicals that either speed up or slow down plant growth. This experiment tested only a few types of liquids and only one kind of seed. You can extend this test to other seeds and other liquids. In fact, if you had enough time, you could track the growth of the seeds until they outgrow their cups. At that point, you could plant them outside and continue the test until they produce their crop. Testing ideas, discovering answers, and testing new ideas are what being a scientist is all about. It's not magic, it's science!

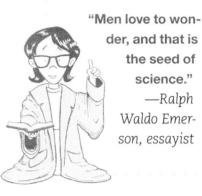

Science Quote

"Men love to wonder, and that is the seed of science."
—Ralph Waldo Emerson, essayist

Science Online

Learn the basics of gardening, even if you have never put a seed in the ground, at **The Garden Helper:** *www .thegardenhelper.com.*

Resources

Web sites

✎www.brainpop.come

✎www.kids.gov/k_science.htm

✎www.sciencemadesimple.com

✎www.sciencenewsforkids

✎www.kids.earth.nasa.gov

✎http://pbskids.org/zoom/activities/sci

✎www.sciencefriday.com/kids

✎www.surfnetkids.com/directory/Science

✎www.pbskids.org/zoom/activities/do/magictricks
.html

Books

Churchill, E. Richard, Louis V. Loeschnig, Muriel Mandell, and Frances Zweifel. *365 Simple Science Experiments* (New York: Sterling Publishing Company, 2000).

Hauser, Jill Frankel, and Michael P. Kline. *Science Play!: Beginning Discoveries for 2- to 6-Year-Olds.* (Charlotte, VT: Williamson Publishing Company, 1998).

Potter, Jean. *Science in Seconds for Kids: Over 100 Experiments You Can Do in Ten Minutes or Less* (San Francisco: Jossey-Bass, 1995).

Magazines

Odyssey Magazine
✎www.odysseymagazine.com

National Geographic Kids
✎www.kids.nationalgeographic.com

YES magazine
✎www.yesmag.bc.ca

Dig: The Archaeology Magazine for Kids
✎www.digonsite.com

Discovery News Online
✎http://dsc.discovery.com/news/news.html

Dragonfly
✎www.units.muohio.edu/dragonfly

The Green Frog News
✎www.thegreenfrognews.com

NWF's Ranger Rick
✎www.nwf.org/rangerrick

Science News for Kids
✎www.sciencenewsforkids.org

Appendix B
Puzzle Answers

ALMOST IMPOSSIBLE • *Page 5*

color this word in yellow

If the word BLUE is colored in yellow, it is almost impossible for your friend to say that the colors of the letters are yellow. They will say blue without thinking, almost every time!

NO ONE CAN SEE 1 • *Page 7*

WHAT D<u>O</u> P<u>I</u>GS USE
T<u>O</u> WR<u>I</u>T<u>E</u>
T<u>O</u>P S<u>E</u>CR<u>E</u>T M<u>E</u>SS<u>A</u>G<u>E</u>S?

NO ONE CAN SEE 2 • *Page 7*

DOWN AND UP • *Page 8*

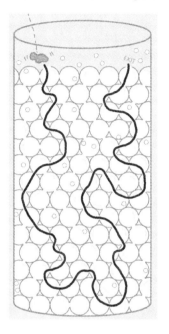

COLD TO HOT??? • *Page 17*

WATER
MATER
ATERM
TAERM
TEARM
TEASM
STEAM

GOING UP • *Page 21*

GOOD CATCH • *Page 29*

	column 1	column 2	column 3
nose	(COLD)	COLD	HOT
arms	COLD	(CATCH)	MUCH
head	(TO)	SLOWER	ARE
twins	THAN	(EASY)	ALWAYS
triplets	THE	HOT	(IS)
thirds	IS	EXACT	(IT)
sun	(BECAUSE)	AT	SAME
double	SPEED	(HOT)	NIGHT

Remember to read the circled words from bottom to top! ↵

THE AMAZING RACE • *Page 37*

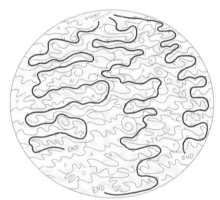

THE EGG GOT BEATEN
THE LETTUCE WAS AHEAD
THE FAUCET KEPT RUNNING

MIX IT UP • *Page 25*

F R O̲ S T̲
H A̲ I L
S N O̲ W S T̲ O̲ R M
I G L O̲ O̲

O̲ V E N
F L̲ A M E
C O̲ A L̲ S
W O̲ O̲ D̲ S T O̲ V E

FIND THE IRON • *Page 39*

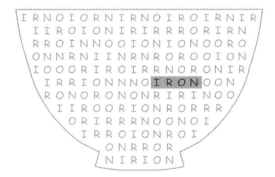

Puzzle Answers

POOF! • *Page 41*

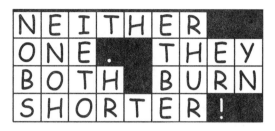

N E I T H E R
O N E .   T H E Y
B O T H   B U R N
S H O R T E R !

WHERE IS THE WATER? • *Page 49*

Where can you find an ocean without water?

OR	X	ON
A	SHOP	X
MOP	X	TOP
AT	MAP	O

DIZZY DROPS • *Page 55*

NEITHER! YOU USE A SEAL!

ABRACADABRA • *Page 51*

How can you make a rock float?

@$P&#&$U>@&#>>T$
&#&$#@&>>I#&$&T@&
$I&$#@@>N#&#>&$$#
#&>$>#A@&#>#&>$>#@&
G#&>L$>#@@A$#@&S$&$
&@#&>W$>#I@@>$T$#&H
#&>$>#@@&#&@$#A&#>
##S@#C&O$@>>O#&P&$
&#O&>$>#@$>##&F@&#
I$C@E$&#C>$R&#E@A M#
$A>@#&>$N&#D>#@@>
S&#O#&#$>#M@$&#E&@
R$O@O&T>&B&#E@E>&#R

TASTE THE DIFFERENCE • *Page 64*

"This <u>lemon</u> tastes awful!" Beth said <u>bitterly</u>.

"I can't eat the <u>chili peppers</u>!" Pam said <u>hotly</u>.

"The <u>sherbet</u> is too cold!" Jan said <u>icily</u>.

"I don't like the <u>pickles</u>!" Ron said <u>sourly</u>.

BLOWING BLUE • Page 65

SAFETY FIRST • Page 81

The most important thing you learn in chemistry class is "Never lick the spoon!"

IMPORTANT INGREDIENT • Page 84

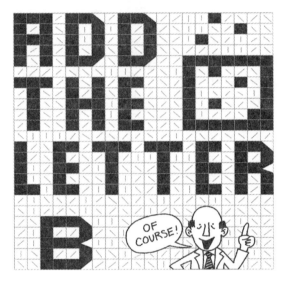

ADD THE ☐ LETTER B

OF COURSE!

SOMETHING IS FISHY • Page 66

YOU CAN TUNE A PIANO, BUT YOU CAN'T TUNA FISH!

OOPS! • Page 90

A. Small bugs that can infect the hair on your head

L I C E
19 27 3 24

B. Flat, square piece of baked clay

T I L E
9 11 6 2

C. To rest on top of water

F L O A T
10 26 4 14 28

D. The opposite of fat

T H I N
18 1 29 8

E. Narrow opening for a coin

S L O T
23 25 16 21

F. Tied hand and foot with rope

B O U N D
15 22 5 30 13

G. Small boo-boo in a car's fender

D E N T
7 20 12 17

Puzzle Answers

OOPS! • *Page 90*

1D H	2B E		3A C	4C O	5F U	6B L	7G D	8D N	' T	9B T
		10C F	11B I	12G N	13F D		14C A			
	15F B	16E O	17G T	18D T	19A L	20G E		21E T	22F O	
23E S	24A E	25E L	26C L		27A I	28C T		29D I	30F N	!

I CAN'T SEE YOU • *Page 111*

When are your eyes not your eyes?

When the wind makes them water!

IT MAKES CENTS • *Page 101*

Move the top penny as shown. This makes two rows that cross each other, and each row has four pennies! Isn't that sneaky?

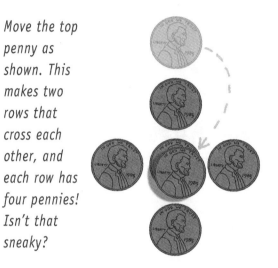

FUNNY FORECAST • *Page 118*

How do you use a rope to tell the weather?

H	A	N	G		I	T		O	U	T		T	H	E
W	I	N	D	O	W	.		I	F		T	H	E	
R	O	P	E		M	O	V	E	S	,		I	T	'	S
W	I	N	D	Y	.		I	F		I	T	'	S	
W	E	T	,		I	T	'	S		R	A	I	N	Y	!

BOWLING WITH AIR • *Page 107*

20 points   29 points   27 points

second turn:
39 points   45 points   42 points

BIG BEANS • *Page 123*

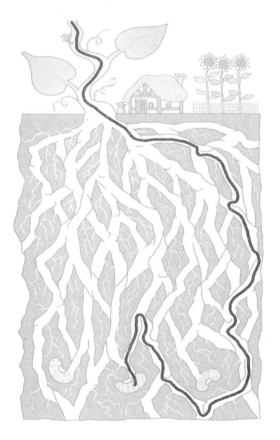

LANDING GEAR • *Page 132*

BECAUSE COLA IS A SOFT DRINK!

MAGIC MATH • *Page 130*

$$\underset{2/3}{H}\ \underset{3/4}{E}\quad \underset{1/4}{A}\ \underset{4/5}{L}\ \underset{3/6}{R}\ \underset{3/4}{E}\ \underset{1/4}{A}\ \underset{1/3}{D}\ \underset{3/8}{Y}\quad \underset{2/5}{K}\ \underset{2/4}{N}\ \underset{3/4}{E}\ \underset{1/5}{W}\quad \underset{2/3}{H}\ \underset{2/2}{O}\ \underset{1/5}{W}$$

$$\underset{1/2}{M}\ \underset{1/4}{A}\ \underset{2/4}{N}\ \underset{3/8}{Y}\quad \underset{2/6}{P}\ \underset{2/2}{O}\ \underset{5/6}{C}\ \underset{2/5}{K}\ \underset{3/4}{E}\ \underset{4/7}{T}\ \underset{3/5}{S}\quad \underset{2/3}{H}\ \underset{3/4}{E}\quad \underset{2/3}{H}\ \underset{1/4}{A}\ \underset{1/3}{D}!$$